清华外文特色系列教材

U0659344

Introduction to Second
Language Acquisition

# 二语习得导论

刘梅华　◇编著

清华大学出版社
北京

## 内 容 简 介

本教材共8个单元，内容涉及母语习得研究、二语习得研究、中介语、二语教学、个体差异与二语习得、社会文化因素与二语习得、二语习得的研究课题和数据类型等，旨在帮助学生了解二语习得所涉及的内容（即语音学和音系学、形态学、句法学、语义学、语用学）、理论（如行为主义理论、天赋论等）、影响因素（如个体差异、社会文化因素等）等，以增加他们对语言学和应用语言学的理解、激发和培养他们对语言学和应用语言学的兴趣。

图书在版编目（CIP）数据

二语习得导论：英文 / 刘梅华编著. —— 北京：清华大学出版社，2025. 6.
(清华外文特色系列教材).

ISBN 978-7-302-68836-5

Ⅰ．H003

中国国家版本馆CIP数据核字第20252RH920号

责任编辑：曹诗悦

封面设计：郑　重

责任校对：王荣静

责任印制：刘海龙

出版发行：清华大学出版社

网　　　址：https://www.tup.com.cn，https://www.wqxuetang.com

地　　　址：北京清华大学学研大厦A座　　邮　　编：100084

社 总 机：010-83470000　　　　　　　　邮　　购：010-62786544

投稿与读者服务：010-62776969, c-service@tup.tsinghua.edu.cn

质量反馈：010-62772015, zhiliang@tup.tsinghua.edu.cn

印 装 者：天津鑫丰华印务有限公司

经　　销：全国新华书店

开　　本：185mm×260mm　　印　　张：11.75　　字　　数：273千字

版　　次：2025 年 6 月第 1 版　　　　　　印　　次：2025 年 6 月第 1 次印刷

定　　价：58.00元

产品编号：099812-01

# 前言

  学习和使用母语之外的其他语言（即二语）不仅仅是个人兴趣，而且有益于个人和社会的发展。学习二语可以拓展个人的思想和行动资源库，促进国际交流和合作，推进国际社会的发展。随着全球化进程的加剧，二语学习者的人数不断增加，学习的语种也越来越多样化，因而，近几十年来，二语教学和研究蓬勃发展。

  二语习得，无论其途径是日常交流还是课堂教学，都需遵循某些原则。这些原则源于人类语言处理的各种特性、学习者的特定动机，以及学习者获取所学语言样本或信息的方式等。二语习得教学和研究的目的是揭示这些原则以及人类语言处理的基本运作信息。本教材是一本介绍二语习得研究的入门书，内容包括母语习得研究、二语习得研究、中介语、二语教学、影响二语习得的各种因素（如学习者个体差异和社会文化因素）等，其读者对象主要是外语专业学生及对二语学习感兴趣的学习者。本教材将阐述关于二语言习得本质的一些基本问题，涉及二语习得的过程、理论和研究方法，并引导学生运用所学以分析一系列问题，旨在拓展并加深学生的专业知识，激发并培养他们对语言学及应用语言学的兴趣。

  本教材共有八个单元，每个单元由三大部分构成：单元目标、知识内容和学习任务。第一单元的主题是语言的本质，简述了语言的特点（如语言的随意性和可变性）和语言的构成——语音（如音素、辅音和元音）、语法（如句子结构和类型）、词汇（如词素和词类）、语义（如词义）和语用（如言语行为理论和会话准则），阐述了研究语言的基本方法（如规范方法与描述方法、共时方法与历时方法）。第二单元的主题是母语习得研究，简述了母语习得的三大理论——行为主义理论（如刺激—反应）、天赋论（如普遍语法、关键期假说）和互动理论（如儿童导向言语），介绍了母语习得的几个阶段（如牙牙学语阶段、单词生成阶段）和几种非典型语言发展（如听力障碍、智力迟钝、失语症、阅读障碍）。第三单元的主题是二语习得研究，介绍了二语习得的一些关键词语（如正式和非正式学习语境），概述了二语习得与母语习得的异同，简述了克拉申（Krashen）的二语习得理论——习得与学习假说、调控假说、自然顺序假说、输入假说和情感过滤假说。

第四单元的主题是中介语，介绍了中介语中的语言僵化现象，概述了语言迁移理论、形式和作用，阐述了二语习得中的语言输入、交际和输出理论及涉及到的重要术语和话题（如反馈），描述了二语习得中的几种知识类型（如陈述性—程序性知识、显性—隐性知识）及影响二语习得的几种心理和认知机制（如注意力、记忆和调控）。第五单元着重于课堂二语教学，涵盖三大内容——课堂环境、教学重点（即以语言形式为主或以意义为主的教学）和教学效果。第六单元的主题是学习者个体差异与二语习得，重点简述了学习者智商、语言能力、态度、学习动机、外语焦虑和学习策略在二语习得中的作用。第七单元关注社会文化因素与二语习得的关系，概述了各种文化（如语言与思维、语言与权力、语言与意识形态、文化适应）和社会因素（如社会阶层、社会关系、性别、区域、行业）对语言习得的影响，并简述了两种社会互动理论——会话分析和社会文化理论。第八单元总结了二语习得研究中的各种可能话题和不同类型的数据，并简述了几种数据分析方法。

随着中国经济和文化的发展，学习二语的人数日益增多。了解二语习得的过程和机制、提高二语习得的成效，不仅有利于个人的全面发展，也有益于增进中国与其他国家和民族的交往和合作，提升中国在国际社会的形象，增强中国在国际社会的话语权。因此，本教材以中国高等教育学习者为对象，旨在概述二语习得教学和研究中的各种现象、课题、理论和方法，为对二语学习感兴趣和有需求的学习者提供一个渠道，以便较为科学、系统地了解语言习得的过程和机制，为进一步学习和研究奠定基础。

本教材融合理论和实证研究结果，深入浅出，激发批判性思维，是国内关于二语习得的为数不多的教材之一。尽管如此，因为语言体系庞大、习得过程复杂、影响因素众多、相关研究数不胜数，本教材只能呈现部分研究的概貌，望广大学习者知悉，并能深入学习、钻研，以便窥见语言习得的本质。

由于编著者水平有限，文中难免有错漏之处，敬请各位读者不吝赐教。

刘梅华

2025年3月于清华园

# Contents

language

culture

learning

hello

world

# The nature of language

## UNIT
## 1

# Objectives

In this unit, you will learn

—the characteristics of language;

—different aspects of language: phonetics and phonology, morphology, syntax, semantics, and pragmatics;

—different approaches to language.

There are approximately 3,000—6,000 distinct languages spoken by humans, and approximately 250 language families, such as the Indo-European language family and the Sino-Tibetan language family. 95% of the world's people speak fewer than 100 of the 6,000 different languages, whereas the last 5% of the world's people speak thousands of discrete languages. Every language has its own way of encoding and expressing human experience, and an entire way of thinking is lost each time a language disappears.

## 1.1 Characteristics of language

Many definitions of language have been proposed. American linguists Bernard Bloch and George L. Trager (1942, cited in Lyons, 1981: 4) stated that "A[a] language is a system of arbitrary vocal symbols by means of which a social group cooperates." Sapir (1921, cited in Lyons, 1981: 3) defined language as "a purely human and non-instinctive method of communicating ideas, emotions and desires by means of voluntarily produced symbols". In a word, language is a system of communication, a tool of thought, a medium for self-expression, a social entity, and so on. It has the following characteristics:

- Language is discrete.
- Language is creative.
- Language is a system.
- Language is arbitrary.
- Language is changeable.

### 1.1.1 Language is discrete

Language is built up from discrete sounds. For example, sounds /s/ and /z/ in English are represented by "s" as in "cats" and "dogs", and sound /l/ is represented by "l" in "love".

*Example 1.1*

Discrete sounds in English: /k/ /ʊ/ /e/ /t/ /d/ /ɪ/ /m/ /f/ /b/ /n/

The number of sounds in a language is limited but varies from language to language. Exchanging such discrete sounds causes a change in the meaning of a signal. For example, /kʊ/ is different from /ke/, and /m/ differs from /en/.

Discreteness means that the boundary between linguistic symbols is clear. Since linguistic symbols are discrete, the chain of linguistic symbols can be segmented until the smallest linguistic symbols are assigned. For example, "She is good" can be divided into subject "she", verb "is" and adjective "good". If the order of these linguistic symbols is changed, the meaning of the sentence becomes completely different, as in "Is she good?". The sentence now is a question instead of a statement.

Clearly, these discrete linguistic symbols of a language can be used repeatedly to combine with other linguistic symbols to express infinite thoughts, which leads to creativity of the language (Irvine, 2014).

### 1.1.2 Language is creative

Chomsky (1972) thinks that language consists of words, rules and interfaces. Among them, rules include syntax, morphology and phonology. Moreover, rules focus on creativity— the ability to produce and understand new language. Rules allow for open-ended creativity, including the expression of unfamiliar meanings and the production of vast numbers of combination.

*Example 1.2*

(1) Daddy is great.

(2) The picture is great.

(3) The show is great.

(4) Daddy eats breakfast.

(5) The picture shows a more scenario of a street.

(6) The show continues an hour and a half.

As indicated by the sentences in Example 1.2, any object can be the subject of a sentence, the subject can have various predicates, followed by diverse adjectives or nouns. Meanwhile, changing the combination of different words can lead to totally different meanings, as shown in Example 1.3.

*Example 1.3*

(1) Is Daddy great?

(2) Is the picture great?

(3) Is the show great?

(4) Does Daddy eat breakfast?

(5) Does the picture show a more scenario of a street?

(6) Does the show continue an hour and a half?

Clearly, language has the potential and creativity to develop infinitely. This is why a child, in spite of the poverty of stimulus, is able to create and understand new words and sentences he or she has never heard before.

Language is a means of expressing an infinite number of thoughts and ideas and can react in an infinite number of ways to new situations. It is creative also because it can adapt to changes in society and technology over time. New words and phrases are created to keep up with changing times. For example, phrases like "surfing the web" and "e-commerce" arose with the spread of the Internet. They were created at a time when the phenomenon occurred and quickly became used by many and recognized by all familiar with the computer.

### 1.1.3   Language is a system

Language is a system of symbols and rules that enable us to communicate (Harley, 2001). The symbols include speech sounds and letters in writing, while the rules include phonology, syntax, and morphology. Both symbols and rules can fall into smaller units that are interdependent on each other. Language is considered as a system primarily because it is made of these discrete yet interdependent linguistic units.

Language is a system also because it is rule-governed. Language has five aspects: phonology, morphonology, syntax, semantics, and pragmatics. Each part is rule-governed in itself:

- phonology—rules for how the language sounds, or should sound,
- morphology—rules for word formation,
- syntax—rules for word order and arrangements,
- semantics—rules of language content, and
- pragmatics—rules of language usage (function and appropriateness).

For example, certain creative formations of sounds are acceptable while others are not permitted, as shown in Example 1.4.

### Example 1.4

(1) grop (√) vs. grpo (x)

(2) fral (√) vs. frla (x)

(3) trast (√) vs. trsat (x)

Similarly, there are special constraints on the meaning and use of particular class of verbs, such as verbs of time expressions (e.g., *winter*, *vacation* and so on) (O'Grady et al., 2011), as shown in Example 1.5.

### Example 1.5

(1) (√) Joe wintered in Michigan.

(2) (√) Jihong vacationed in Dalian.

(3) (x) Sally nooned in a hotel.

(4) (x) George five minuted in the shop.

It is clear that when a verb is created from a time expression, it must indicate a period of time. Hence, "Joe wintered in Michigan" means "Joe was in Michigan for the winter", and "Jihong vacationed in Dalian" means "Jihong was in Dalian for the vacation". Since "noon" and "minute" express "points in time" rather than "a period of time", they cannot be used as verbs in such a creative way.

Evidently, in order for language to work, we need a way to say words (phonology), to know the meaning attached to these words (morphology), to understand the meanings of words combined within a sentence (syntax), and how greater the non-verbal context informs of the meaning of language (pragmatics). These different systems work in conjunction to make it easy and automatic to produce and understand a sentence or an utterance. This is especially clear when one tries to learn a new language and realizes how many different pieces he or she has to learn before he or she moves to navigate the language.

These systems are discrete and interdependent. Each system has sub-systems, yet they become fully meaningful only when they work together. This is why we say language is a "system of systems" (Mulder & Hervey, 1975). It is impossible to think of spoken language without phonology, the individual sounds that make up words. These sounds would become meaningless if they did not correspond to words that we understand as meaningful. Likewise, language would be incredibly limited if we had words but no way to pronounce them.

The ability to handle new utterances is best demonstrated in the production and comprehension of utterances/sentences. Every day, we are exposed to numerous novel combinations of words, ideas and information that we have never heard, read or said before.

### 1.1.4    Language is arbitrary

Language is arbitrary. This is because language is based on arbitrary symbols. Words have no inherent relation to the objects, people, and commands they stand for. For example, "chair" refers to the object that people can sit on, "pan" refers to the object that people use to fry food, and so on. The relationship between these signifiers (a form such as a sound, morpheme, word, phrase, clause, or sign like "chair" and "pan") and the signified (an object, action, quality, or quantity) is arbitrary, but not planned or objective (Monaghan et al., 2014).

Language is arbitrary also because different sounds from different languages may convey the same meaning. For example, "water" (English), "eau" (French), "agua" (Spanish), and "shuǐ" (Chinese) all mean water. Also, same sounds from different languages may convey different meanings, such as "knee" (English), "nie" ("never" in German), and "nǐ" ("you" in Chinese).

### 1.1.5    Language is changeable

Language is always changing. It changes across space, across social groups, and across time. Language change has many types, including sound changes, lexical changes, semantic changes, and syntactic changes.

Generation by generation, pronunciations evolve, new words are borrowed or invented, the meaning of old words drifts, and morphology develops or decays. A typical example in sound change that occurred between Middle and Early Modern English (around Shakespeare's time) is known as the Great Vowel Shift. At that time, there was a length distinction in the English vowels, and the Great Vowel Shift altered the position of all the long vowels, in a giant rotation. The nucleus of the two high vowels (front "long ɪ" /i:/, and the back "long ʊ" /ʊ:/) started to drop, and the high position was retained only in the offglide. Eventually, the original /i:/ became /ai/, so the "long i:" vowel in Modern English is now pronounced /ai/ as in the word "bite" (/bait/). Similarly, the "long ʊ:" dropped all the way to /aʊ/. So, the earlier /hʊ:s/ of "house" became /haʊs/.

All natural languages change. This happens for several reasons. First, language changes because the needs of its speakers change. New technologies, new products, and new experiences require new words to refer to them clearly and efficiently. So, new words and phrases like "Internet", "website", "homepage", "e-commerce", and "surf the Internet" emerged as technology developed. Another example is the word "text". Originally it was used as in "text message" to show that one person sent another text rather than voice messages by phone. Gradually, people began using the shorter form "text" to refer to both the message and the process, as in "I got a text from my sister" or "He has already texted John".

Another reason for language change is that no two people have had exactly the same language experience because of age, job, education level, region of the country, and so on. We pick up new words and phrases from all the different people we talk to. We borrow them from other languages (e.g., "sushi" and "tea"), we create them by shortening longer words (e.g., "gym" from "gymnasium", "hippo" from "hippopotamus") or by combining words (e.g., "brunch" from "breakfast", "lunch" and "snark" from "snake" and "shark"), and we make them out of proper names (e.g., "Levis" and "Fahrenheit").

The rate of change varies. Many factors influence the rate at which language changes, including speakers' attitudes toward borrowing and change (Ottenheimer, 2009). When most members of a speech community value novelty, their language will change more quickly. When most members of a speech community value stability, then their language will change more slowly. When a particular pronunciation, word, grammatical form, or turn of phrase is regarded as more desirable, or marks its users as more important or powerful, then it will be adopted and imitated more rapidly.

The branch of linguistics that is expressly concerned with changes in a language over time is **historical linguistics,** also known as **diachronic linguistics**.

## 1.2 Aspects of language

Language has five aspects: phonetics and phonology, morphonology, syntax, semantics, and pragmatics.

### 1.2.1 Phonetics and phonology

#### 1.2.1.1 Phonetics

Phonetics is the study of the sounds of language. Phonetics is divided into three types according to the production (articulatory), transmission (acoustic), and perception (auditive) of sounds: acoustic phonetics, auditory phonetics and articulatory phonetics.

- Acoustic phonetics is the study of the physical properties of sounds.

- Auditory phonetics is the study of the way listeners perceive sounds.

- Articulatory phonetics is the study of how the vocal tracts produce the sounds. It is related to the articulatory movements in the chest, throat, mouth, and nose which produce them.

Sounds in English are classified into consonants and vowels. Table 1.1 presents English phonemic symbols that are used in this textbook.

**Table 1.1   English phonemic symbols** (Field, 2007)

| Consonants | | | | Vowels | | | |
|---|---|---|---|---|---|---|---|
| **Voiceless** | | **Voiced** | | **Short** | | **Long** | |
| **Stops/Plosives** | | | | ɪ | *bit* | i: | *beat* |
| p | *pit* | b | *bit* | e | *let* | ɑ: | *far* |
| t | *tar* | d | *dot* | æ | *bad* | ɔ: | *fort* |
| k | *kite* | g | *get* | ʌ | *hut* | ʊ: | *boot* |
| **Fricatives** | | | | ɔ | *hot* | ə: | *hurt* |
| f | *fat* | v | *vet* | ʊ | *put* | | |
| θ | *thin* | ð | *the* | ə | *ago* | | |
| s | *sit* | z | *zeal* | | | | |
| ʃ | *ship* | ʒ | *treasure* | **Diphthongs** | | | |
| h | *ham* | | | ei | *late* | aʊ | *loud* |
| **Affricates** | | | | ai | *like* | ɪə | *here* |
| ʧ | *chat* | ʤ | *bridge* | ɔi | *soil* | eə | *where* |
| **Nasals** | | | | əʊ | *boat* | ʊə | *lure* |
| | | m | *map* | | | | |
| | | n | *nose* | **Triphthongs** | | | |
| | | ŋ | *tongue* | aiə | *hire* | aʊə | *flower* |
| **Approximants** | | | | | | | |
| | | w | *we* | | | | |
| | | r | *rip* | | | | |
| | | j | *yet* | | | | |
| **Lateral** | | | | | | | |
| | | l | *lap* | | | | |

## I. Consonants

Consonants are produced as air from the lungs is pushed through the glottis (the opening between the vocal cords) and out of the mouth. They are classified according to voicing, aspiration, nasal/oral sounds, places of articulation and manners of articulation. Voicing is whether the vocal folds vibrate or not. The sound /s/ is called voiceless because there is no vibration, and the sound /z/ is called voiced because the vocal folds do vibrate. Only three sounds in English have aspiration: /b/, /p/ and /t/. An extra puff of air is pushed out when these sounds begin a word or stressed syllable. Hold a piece of paper close to your mouth when you are saying the words "pin" and "spin". You should notice extra air when you say "pin".

Aspiration is indicated in writing with a superscript "h", as in $/p^h/$. Nasal sounds are produced when the velum (the soft palate located in the back of the roof of the mouth) is lowered and air is passed through the nose and mouth. Oral sounds are produced when the velum is raised and air passes only through the mouth.

### A. Places of articulation

According to places of articulation, consonants can be labial, bilabial, labiodental, dental, interdental, alveolar, alveopalatal/postalveolar, palatal, velar, glottal, or labiovelar.

- Labial: Any sound made with closure or near-closure of the lips.

- Bilabial: Sounds involving both lips—/p/ /b/ /m/.

- Labiodental: Sounds involving the lower lip and upper/front teeth—/f/ /v/.

- Dental: Sounds produced with the tongue placed against or near the teeth.

- Interdental: Tongue placed between the upper and the lower teeth—/θ/ /ð/.

- Alveolar: Tongue near the alveolar ridge on roof of the mouth (in between the teeth and the hard palate) (Within the oral cavity, a small ridge protrudes from just behind the upper front teeth, which is called the alveolar ridge)—/t/ /d/ /s/ /z/ /l/ /n/.

- Alveopalatal/Postalveolar: The roof of the mouth rises sharply just behind the alveolar ridge (tongue towards soft palate)—/ʃ/ /ʒ/ /tʃ/ /dʒ/.

- Palatal: Tongue on the hard palate (the highest part of the roof of the mouth is called palate)—/j/.

- Velar: Tongue near the velum (the soft area toward the rear of the mouth is called the velum)—/k/ /g/ /ŋ/.

- Glottal: Space between vocal folds—/h/.

- Labiovelar: Tongue raised near the velum and the lips rounded at the same time—/w/.

### B. Manners of articulation

According to manners of articulation, consonants can be grouped as oral, nasal, stop, fricative, affricate, approximant, liquid and lateral.

- Oral vs. nasal phones: When the velum is raised, cutting the airflow through the nasal passages, oral sounds are produced. The velum can also be lowered to allow air to pass through the nasal passages, producing a sound that is nasal.

- Stops: Obstruct the airstream completely.

- Fricatives: The airstream is partially obstructed and a turbulent airflow is produced.

- Affricates: Stop the airstream, then release it.

- Approximants: Consonant sounds produced by complete or partial closure of the vocal tract, similar to a fast vowel.

- Liquid: A consonant sound in which the tongue produces a partial closure in the mouth, resulting in a resonant, vowel-like consonant, such as English /l/ and /r/.

- Laterals: Consonant sounds produced with the airflow around the sides of the tongue, such as varieties of /l/.

One should practice saying the sounds of the English alphabet to see if they can identify the places of articulation in the mouth. The sounds are described by voicing, place of articulation, and then manner of articulation. For example, the sound /j/ is called a voiced palatal glide and the sound /s/ is called a voiceless alveolar fricative.

**Table 1.2   Features of consonants in English**

|  | Bilabial | Labiodental | Interdental | Alveolar | Postalveolar | Palatal | Velar | Glottal |
|---|---|---|---|---|---|---|---|---|
| Stop/Plosive | p<br>b |  |  | t<br>d |  |  | k<br>g |  |
| Nasal (stop) | m |  |  | n |  |  | ŋ |  |
| Fricative |  | f<br>v | θ<br>ð | s<br>z | ʃ<br>ʒ |  |  | h |
| Affricate |  |  |  |  | tʃ<br>dʒ |  |  |  |
| Approximant | w |  |  |  |  | j |  |  |
| Lateral approximant |  |  |  | l |  |  |  |  |

## II. Vowels

Vowels are produced by holding the tongue in certain positions and letting the airstream pass over it without any kind of interruption or friction. Most vowels are voiced (vowels in English are all voiced, while Japanese has voiceless vowels). They are classified according to the height of the tongue, the part of the tongue involved, and the position of the lips. The tongue can be high, middle, or low; and the part of the tongue used can be front, central, or back. Generally, long vowels are tense and short vowels are lax. Hence, the sound /ɪ/ can be written as a front, high, lax, unrounded vowel.

Many languages also have vowels called diphthongs, a sequence of two vowel sounds. Examples in English include /ɔi/ in "boy" and /aʊ/ in "cow". English also has triphthongs—a sequence of three vowel sounds, such as /aiə/ in "fire" and /aʊə/ in "sour".

In addition, vowels can be nasalized when they occur before nasal consonants. A diacritic mark [~] is placed over the vowel to show this. The vowel sound [i:] in the word "lean" is considered different because the sound in "lean" is nasalized [ĩ:].

**Table 1.3    Features of cardinal vowels in English**

| | | Part of tongue | | | |
| --- | --- | --- | --- | --- | --- |
| | | Front | Central | Back | |
| **Tongue height** | High/Close | i: <br> ɪ | | ʊ: <br> ʊ | Rounded/ Unrounded |
| | Close-mid <br> Open-mid | e | ə <br> ʌ | ɔ: <br> ɔ | |
| | Low/Open | æ | | ɑ: | |

In writing, "[ ]" is often used to transcribe speech sounds, as shown in Example 1.6.

***Example 1.6***

leaf [li:f]    cut [kʌt]    book [bʊk]    close [kləʊs]

sip [sɪp]    bridge [brɪdʒ]    glass [glɑ:s]    three [θri:]

### 1.2.1.2    Phonology

**Phonology** is the study of the speech sounds of a language and the laws governing them. It describes the way sounds function within a given language and operates at the level of sound systems and abstract sound units. Knowing the sounds of a language is only a small part of phonology. This importance is shown by the fact that one can change one word into another by simply changing one sound.

### Ⅰ. Phoneme

Consider the differences between the words "time" and "dime": The words are identical except for the first sound. /t/ and /d/ can therefore distinguish words, and are called contrasting sounds. All distinctive sounds are classified as phonemes. **Phoneme** is the smallest unit of speech distinguishing one word from another, as the element /p/ in "tap", which separates "tap" from words "tab", "tag", and "tan".

Phonemes are based on spoken language and are conventionally recorded between slash marks "/ /". The full set of phonemes (contrastive sets) of a language is called the phonemic system of that language (see Table 1.1 for the phonemic symbols in English). Table 1.4 presents the list of phonemic symbols commonly used to show the possible initial and final consonant contrasts in English utterances, with examples (Wardhaugh, 1977).

#### Table 1.4    Initial and final consonant phonemes in English

| Initial | Examples | Final | Examples |
|---------|----------|-------|----------|
| /p/ | pit | /p/ | lap |
| /b/ | bit | /b/ | lab |
| /t/ | Tim | /t/ | cat |
| /d/ | dim | /d/ | cad |
| /k/ | kit | /k/ | back |
| /g/ | git | /g/ | bag |
| /f/ | fast | /f/ | leaf |
| /v/ | vast | /v/ | leave |
| /ð/ | that | /ð/ | seethe |
| /ʃ/ | ship | /z/ | rise |
| /s/ | sip | /s/ | rice |
| /z/ | zip | /ʃ/ | crash |
| /ʧ/ | chin | /ʧ/ | teach |
| /θ/ | thin | /θ/ | mirth |
| /dʒ/ | gin | /dʒ/ | merge |
| /m/ | meat | /m/ | cram |
| /n/ | neat | /n/ | ran |
| /h/ | heat | /ŋ/ | rang |
| /l/ | let | /l/ | seal |
| /r/ | red | /r/ | seer |
| /j/ | yet | | |
| /w/ | wed | | |

Phonemes are not physical sounds. They are abstract mental representations of the phonological units of a language. **Phones** are considered to be any single speech sound of which phonemes are made. Phonemes are a family of phones regarded as a single sound and represented by the same symbol. The different phones that are the realization of a phoneme are called **allophones** of that phoneme. The use of allophones is not random, but rule-governed. No one is taught these rules as they are learned subconsciously when the native language is acquired. To distinguish between a phoneme and its allophones, slashes "/ /" are used to enclose phonemes and brackets "[ ]" to indicate allophones or phones. For example, [ɪ] and [ĩ] are allophones of the phoneme /ɪ/; [p] and [pʰ] are allophones of the phoneme /p/.

Allophones are usually relatively similar sounds which are in mutually exclusive or complementary distribution (C.D.). The C.D. of two phones means that the two phones can never be found in the same environment (i.e., the same environment in the sense of position in the word and the identity of adjacent phonemes). If two sounds are phonetically similar and are in C.D., then they can be assumed to be allophones of the same phoneme.

If two sounds are allophones of the same phoneme, they are said to be in complementary distribution. These sounds cannot occur in minimal pairs and they cannot change the meaning of otherwise identical words. When two sounds always occur in different environments and never occur in the same environment, they are in complementary distribution, like [p] in "pit" and "sip".

**Minimal pairs** are words with different meanings that have the same sounds except for one. These contrasting sounds can either be consonants or vowels. For example, the words "pin" and "bin" are minimal pairs because they are exactly the same except for the first sound. The words "read" and "rude" are also exactly the same except for the vowel sound. Words "time" and "dime" are also minimal pairs.

Apparently, words with one contrastive sound are minimal pairs. Another feature of minimal pairs is their overlapping distribution. Sounds that occur in phonetic environments that are identical are said to be in overlapping distribution. The sounds of [ɪn] from "pin" and "bin" are in overlapping distribution because they occur in both words. The same is true for the sounds of [θr] in "three" and "through".

Nasalized vowels are allophones of the same phoneme in English, such as the sounds in "fat" and "fan". The phoneme is /æ/, however, the allophones are [æ] and [æ̃]. Yet in French, nasalized vowels are not allophones of the same phonemes. They are separate phonemes. The words "beau" [bo] and "bon" [bõ] are not in complementary distribution because they are minimal pairs and have contrasting sounds. In this case, changing the sounds changes the meaning of the words.

### Ⅱ. Syllable

A **syllable** is a unit of organization for a sequence of speech sounds. It is typically made up of a syllable nucleus (most often a vowel) with optional initial and final margins (often consonants). Syllables are often thought of as the phonological "building blocks" of words. They can influence the rhythm, prosody, poetic metre and stress patterns of a language.

The general structure of a syllable (σ) consists of three segments. These segments are grouped into two components: onset and rime.

- Onset (ω): Consists of a consonant or consonant cluster at the beginning of a syllable, before the nucleus. It is obligatory in some languages, optional or even restricted in others. Syllables without an onset may be said to have a zero onset.

- Rime (ρ): Consists of nucleus and coda.

Nucleus (ν) consists of a vowel or syllabic consonant in the middle of a syllable, and is obligatory in most languages. Coda (κ) consists of a consonant or consonant cluster after the nucleus. It is optional in some languages, highly restricted or prohibited in others.

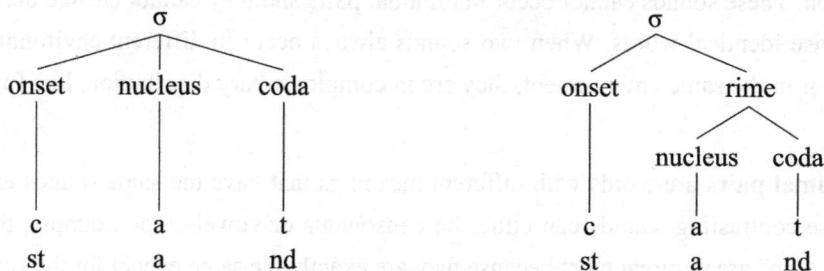

**Figure 1.1   Syllable structure**

A word can consist of a single syllable, which is called a **monosyllable**, like English words "dog", "peak", "fire" and "book". There may be more than one syllable in a word: **bisyllable** for a word of two syllables (e.g., "vowel", "teller" and "onset"), **trisyllable** for a word of three syllables (e.g., "beautiful" and "possible"), and **polysyllable** for a word of more than three syllables or for any word of more than one syllable (e.g., "understatement" and "prolific").

### III. Suprasegmental unit

**Suprasegmental units** refer to the nonlinear units of language that are superimposed on segmental units. Such suprasegmental units of language as syllables, words, and phrases are distinguished during the sequential linear segmentation of the spoken chain. Suprasegmental units of language include such prosodic elements as length, stress, tone, melody, rhythm, and intonation, as well as markers indicating the juncture of segmental units.

### A. Stress

Stress is a property of a whole syllable. The stress level of a syllable can only be determined by comparing it with neighboring syllables which have more or less stress. Word stress is the accent on a syllable within a word, for example:

'beautiful          'fight          tra'dition          acci'dental          'accent

Stress is often used to distinguish between otherwise identical words: English words "'content" means "what is about...", and "con'tent" means "satisfied"; Spanish words "término" means "term" while "termíno" means "I terminate" and "terminó" means "he terminated".

Sentence stress is the accent on certain words within a sentence, which are often content words.

### Example 1.7

(1) I sell my car because I'll go to France.

(2) Will you sell my car because I'll go to France?

**B. Tone**

Both words and utterances show pitch/tone variations during the process of production.

### Example 1.8

(1) John came.

(2) John came?

(3) "John came," I said.

These three utterances of Example 1.8 are different because of the way the pitch of the voice falls on "came" in Sentence (1), rises on "came" in Sentence (2), and stays level on "came" in Sentence (3).

There are generally four tone/pitch levels—/1/, /2/, /3/, /4/: /4/ indicates the highest pitch level, /1/ the lowest, and /3/ and /2/ the intermediate levels. In Mandarin Chinese, tone/pitch is a distinctive suprasegmental feature. For example, /shi/ pronounced on a high, level note means "to lose", on a slight rising note means "ten", on a falling note means "city, market", and on a falling-rising note means "history". /ma/ with a high, level pitch means "mother", but with a falling-rising note means "horse".

### C. Juncture

Junctures are pauses between words to show differences in meaning:

### Example 1.9

(1) nitrate

(2) night rate

(3) nye trait

The juncture phoneme apparently demonstrates a significant pause, which distinguishes the three utterances. Similarly, English phrases "beer dripped" and "beard ripped" are distinguished by word juncture.

## 1.2.2 Morphology

**Morphology** is the study of the internal structure of words.

### 1.2.2.1 Morpheme

**Morphemes** are the minimal units of words that have a meaning and cannot be subdivided further. Morphemes are not equivalent to what we conventionally regard as words. For example, "cats" is one word but has two morphemes: "cat" and "plural-s".

There are two main types of morphemes: free morphemes and bound morphemes. Free morphemes can stand alone (a word by itself); bound morphemes cannot stand alone with meaning and must be attached to other elements to form words.

*Example 1.10*

| free morphemes/words: | bed | bad | friend | book | smile |
|---|---|---|---|---|---|
| bound morphemes: | -ly | -less | un- | im- | -er |
| words: | sadly | careless | unlike | impossible | bigger |

Morphemes are comprised of two separate classes: bases (or roots) and affixes. A "**base**", or "**root**" is a morpheme in a word that gives the word its principal meaning. An example of a free base morpheme is "woman" in the word "womanly". An example of a bound base morpheme is "-sent" in the word "dissent".

An "**affix**" is a bound morpheme that occurs before or after a base. An affix that comes before a base is called a "**prefix**". Some examples of prefixes are "ante-", "pre-", "un-", and "dis-", as in the following words:

**ante**date        **pre**historic

**un**likely        **dis**respect

An affix that comes after a base is called a "**suffix**". Some examples of suffixes are "-ly", "-er", "-ism", and "-ment", as in the following words:

angri**ly**        work**er**

material**ism**    state**ment**

An affix can be either derivational or inflectional. "**Derivational affixes**" serve to alter the meaning of a word by building on a base. They are added to morphemes to form new words, which may or may not be the same part of speech. In the examples of words with prefixes and suffixes above, the addition of the prefix "un-" to "unlikely" alters the meaning of "likely". The resulting word means "not likely". The addition of the suffix "-er" to "work" changes the meaning of "work", which is an act of doing something, to a word that refers to "a person who works". Derivational affix can be added to derivational affix. For example, judge–judgment–judgmental, arm–rearm–antirearm.

### Table 1.5　Some derivational affixes in English

| Affix | Change | Examples |
|---|---|---|
| **Suffixes** | | |
| -able | verb→adjective | read·able, understand·able, fix·able |
| -ing | verb→adjective | writ·ing pad, work·ing memeory |
| -ive | verb→adjective | impress·ive, submiss·ive, assert·ive |
| -al | verb→noun | dispos·al, refus·al |
| -ant | verb→noun | defend·ant, particip·ant |
| -(at)ion | verb→noun | protect·ion, act·ion, assumpt·ion |
| -er(or) | verb→noun | work·er, sing·er, act·or |
| -ment | verb→noun | state·ment, amuse·ment, judge·ment |
| -dom | noun→noun | king·dom, queen·dom |
| -ful | noun→adjective | care·ful, faith·ful, hope·ful |
| -(i)al | noun→adjective | nation·al, form·al |
| -(i)an | noun→adjective | Asi·an, Americ·an |
| -ic | noun→adjective | stat·ic, optimist·ic |
| -less | noun→adjective | care·less, hope·less |
| -ous | noun→adjective | poison·ous, marvell·ous |
| -ize | noun→verb | material·ize, capital·ize |
| -ish | adjective→adjective | green·ish, black·ish |
| -ate | adjective→verb | active·ate, rejuven·ate |
| -en | adjective→verb | hard·en, flat·ten |
| -ize | adjective→verb | modern·ize, real·ize, final·ize |
| -ly | adjective→adverb | slow·ly, quick·ly, strong·ly |
| -ness | adjective→noun | happi·ness, sad·ness, weak·ness |
| -ity | adjective→noun | prior·ity, acceptabil·ity |
| **Prefixes** | | |
| anti- | noun→noun | anti·body, anti·virus |
| ex- | noun→noun | ex·wife, ex·president |
| de- | verb→verb | de·activate, de·mute |
| dis- | verb→verb | dis·obey, dis·connect, dis·please |
| mis- | verb→verb | mis·place, mis·use |
| re- | verb→verb | re·do, re·write, re·take |
| un- | verb→verb | un·do, un·lock |
| in- | adjective→adjective | in·complete, in·compatible |
| un- | adjective→adjective | un·happy, un·fair |
| im- | adjective→adjective | im·possible, im·perceptible |

It should be noted that all prefixes in English are derivational. However, suffixes may be either derivational or inflectional.

**Inflectional affixes** are added to the end of an existing word for purely grammatical reasons. There are a large number of derivational affixes in English. But there are only eight "inflectional affixes", which are all suffixes except in irregular forms: men (middle), deer (no change). As presented in Table 1.6, inflectional affixes tend to be morphemes with meanings such as "plural", "possessive", and "past tense".

**Table 1.6   Inflectional affixes in English**

| Inflectional affix | Meaning | Examples |
|---|---|---|
| -s | 3rd person singular present | She waits. |
| -ed | past tense | She walked. |
| -ing | progressive | She is walking. |
| -en | past participle | She has forgotten. |
| -s | plural | She eats three tables. |
| -'s | possessive | John's table |
| -er | comparative | happier |
| -est | superlative | happiest |

#### 1.2.2.2   Types of words

There are two groups of words: lexical (or content) words and function (or grammatical) words. Lexical words are called open-class words and include nouns, verbs, adjectives, and adverbs. Function words, or closed-class words, are conjunctions, prepositions, articles, and pronouns. New words can regularly be added to lexical words and cannot be (or are very rarely) added to function words.

Words can be classified into antonyms, hyponyms, and metonyms based on their relationships in meaning.

- Antonyms: Words that are opposite in meaning, like "big" and "small".

- Hyponyms: A set of related words. For example, "red", "white", "yellow", and "blue" are all hyponyms of "color".

- Metonyms: Words used in place of another to convey the same meaning (e.g., "jock" for "athlete", "Washington" for "American government", "crown" for "monarch").

### 1.2.3   Syntax

**Syntax** refers to the rules that govern the ways in which words combine to form phrases, clauses, and sentences, or the study of the syntactic properties of a language. The following statements apply to syntax:

- Syntax is the proper order of words in a phrase or sentence.

- Syntax is a tool for writing proper grammatical sentences.

- Native speakers of a language learn correct syntax without realizing it.

- The complexity of a writer's or speaker's sentences creates a formal or informal level of diction that is presented to its audience.

Syntax often depends on lexical categories (parts of speech). Generally speaking, there are eight main parts of speech: noun, verb, adjective, adverb, determiner, auxiliary verb, preposition, and conjunction.

### 1.2.3.1   Phrase structure rules

Phrase structure rules describe how phrases are formed and in what order, as shown in Table 1.7.

**Table 1.7   Phrase structure rules in English**

| Noun phrase (NP) | (Determiner) (adjective) noun (PP) |
|---|---|
| Verb phrase (VP) | Verb (NP) (PP) |
| Prepositional phrase (PP) | Preposition NP |
| Sentence (S) | NP VP |

### 1.2.3.2   Sentences

The following statements are true about sentences in English:

- A new sentence begins with a capital letter. For example,

  He (capital letter) obtained his degree.

- A sentence ends with punctuation (a period, a question mark, or an exclamation point). For example,

  He obtained his degree. (period)

- A sentence contains a subject that is only given once. For example,

  Smith (subject) obtained his degree.

- A sentence contains a verb or a verb phrase. For example,

  He obtained (verb) his degree.

- A sentence follows "Subject + Verb + Object" word order. For example,

  He (subject) obtained (verb) his degree (object).

- A sentence must have a complete idea that stands alone. This is also called an independent clause. For example,

  He obtained his degree.

Generally speaking, there are four main types of sentences: declarative sentence, command or imperative sentence, question or interrogative sentence, and exclamatory sentence, as shown in Example 1.11.

**Example 1.11**

(1) This flower is beautiful. (declarative)

(2) Give me the flower. (command)

(3) Is this flower beautiful? (question)

(4) What a beautiful flower it is! (exclamation)

A sentence is often made up of clauses. There are two types of clauses: independent clauses and dependent clauses. An independent clause can stand alone as a sentence. It contains a subject and a verb and expresses a complete idea. A dependent clause is not a complete sentence. It must be attached to an independent clause to become complete. It is thus also known as a subordinate clause.

In terms of structure, there are simple, compound, complex, and compound-complex sentences.

- Simple sentence: Contains a subject and a verb. It may also have an object and modifiers. However, it contains only **one** independent clause.

- Compound sentence: Contains at least **two** independent clauses. These two independent clauses can be joined by a comma and a coordinating conjunction, or by a semicolon.

- Complex sentence: Contains at least **one** independent clause and at least **one** dependent clause. Dependent clauses can refer to the subject (*who, which*), the sequence/time (*since, while*), or the causal elements (*because, if*) of the independent clause.

- Compound-complex sentence: Contains at least **two** independent clauses and at least **one** dependent clause.

*Example 1.12*

(1) She completed her literature review. (simple)

(2) She completed her literature review, <u>and</u> she created her reference list. (compound)

(3) <u>Because</u> he organized his sources by theme, it was easier for his readers to follow. (complex)

(4) She completed her literature review, <u>but</u> she still needs to work on her methods section <u>even though</u> she finished her methods course last semester. (compound-complex)

(5) <u>Although</u> he organized his sources by theme, George decided to arrange them chronologically, <u>and</u> he carefully followed the MEAL plan for organization. (compound-complex)

(6) They studied APA rules for many hours <u>as</u> they were so interesting. (complex)

(7) He organized his sources by theme; <u>then,</u> he updated his reference list. (compound)

### 1.2.4  Semantics

**Semantics** refers to the study of relationships between words and how we construct meaning. It is about the meaning of words, phrases, and sentences. Semantics largely determines our reading comprehension, how we understand others, and even what decisions we make as a result of our interpretations.

Lexical semantics is concerned with the meaning of words and the meaning of relationships among words. Phrasal semantics is concerned with the meaning of syntactic units larger than the word.

Semantic properties are the components of the meanings of words. For example, the semantic property "human" can be found in many words such as "parent", "doctor", "baby", "professor", "widow", and "aunt". Other semantic properties include animate objects, male, female, countable items, and non-countable items.

Thematic roles are the semantic relationships between the verbs and noun phrases of sentences. Table 1.8 shows the thematic roles in relation to the verbs of sentences.

**Table 1.8    Thematic roles in sentences**

| Thematic role | Description | Example |
|---|---|---|
| Agent | The one who performs an action | *Mary* jumped. |
| Theme | The person or thing that undergoes an action | John called *Mary*. |
| Location | The place where an action takes place | It rains in *France*. |
| Goal | The place to which an action is directed | Put the cat *in the basket*. |

(Continued)

| Thematic role | Description | Example |
|---|---|---|
| Source | The place from which an action originates | John flew from *Detroit* to San Diego. |
| Instrument | The means by which an action is performed | John cuts his hair *with scissors*. |
| Experiencer | One who perceives something | *Mary* heard the child play violin. |
| Causative | A natural force that causes a change | *The flood* destroyed the houses. |
| Possessor | One who has something | A picture of *John* was lost. |
| Recipient | One who receives something | I gave it to *my mom*. |

The meaning of sentences is constructed from the meaning of noun phrases and verbs. Sentences contain truth conditions if the circumstances in the sentences are true. Paraphrases are two sentences with the same truth conditions, despite subtle differences in structure and emphasis. "The ball was kicked by the boy" is a paraphrase of the sentence "The boy kicked the ball", but they have the same truth conditions that a boy kicked a ball.

Sometimes the truth of one proposition entails or implies the truth of another proposition. This is called entailment and its opposite is called contradiction, where one proposition implies the falseness of another. For example, "He was assassinated" entails that he is dead. "He was assassinated" contradicts the statement "He is alive".

Generally speaking, words, phrases and sentences have referential, connotative, and conceptual meanings.

- Referential meaning: Knowing the reference of words. For example, in English, a "table" refers to an object with a flat top and either three or four legs, and a "leaf" most often refers to part of a tree.

- Connotative meaning: The meaning or relationship of meanings of a sign or set of signs.

### Example 1.13

(1) The boy bit the dog.

(2) The dog bit the boy.

Sentences in Example 1.13 share the same structure but different meanings. This demonstrates that syntax and meaning interrelate.

- Conceptual meaning: Logical, cognitive, or denotative content of words, phrases, or sentences. It is based on two structural principles, which are contractiveness and constituent structures (in a scientific way). It is usually derived from definitions we find in dictionaries and the appearance of these lexical items. We give these lexical items features (constituent structures) and eliminate other features which are not present (contractiveness structures). For example, the word "woman" could be specified as (+ human, + adult, – male). It is distinct from "man", which could be defined (+ human, + adult, + male). "Man" is incompatible with "woman" because of the distinct feature—male feature.

Note that semantics does not necessarily correspond to grammaticality because many ungrammatical sentences are meaningful, or at least interpretable, as shown in Example 1.14.

### Example 1.14

(1) That woman beautiful is my mother.

(2) I'll happy if I can get your paper.

(3) That bachelor is married.

Sentences (1) and (2) of Example 1.14 as well as many other sentences that are uttered by non-native speakers of English are perfectly comprehensible, despite the fact that they do not follow the "rules" of English. The reverse side of the picture is the sentence that is grammatically correct but meaningless in content (at least without additional contextualization), as shown in Example 1.14 Sentence (3).

### 1.2.5   Pragmatics

**Pragmatics** is the study of how context affects meaning, such as how sentences are interpreted in certain situations (or the interpretation of linguistic meaning in context). Linguistic context is the discourse that precedes the sentence being interpreted, and situational context is knowledge about the world.

For example, in the sentence "The kids have eaten already and surprisingly, they are hungry", the linguistic context helps to interpret the second clause depending on what the first clause says. The situational context helps to interpret the second clause because it is common knowledge that humans are usually not hungry after eating.

#### 1.2.5.1   Speech act theory

To understand language use in context and account for the speaker's and the addressee's verbal and non-verbal contributions to the negotiation of meaning in interaction, Austin (1962) introduced the **speech act theory**, which views language as a sort of action rather than as a medium for communication and expression. The theory emphasizes that utterances have different or specific meanings to their users and listeners other than their literal meanings according to the language. The theory further identifies that there are two kinds of utterances: constative and performative utterances.

**Constative utterances** describe states of affairs that are either true or false. They are utterances which describe the world and in doing so ascertain or state something. Constatives are mostly (though not necessarily) in the form of declarative sentences. They refer to the act of saying something, and are truth-evaluable or at least purport to describe reality (Petrey, 1990).

*Example 1.15*

(1) Snow is white. (true)

(2) Snow is red. (false)

A constative utterance performs the following functions:

- It conveys a message;

- The message can be compared to the real world and declared true or false;

- A failed constative is false, unclear, or void of reference (i.e., the thing it's talking about doesn't exist).

*Example 1.16*

(1) Mia's hair is now black.

(2) Critics speculate that Friedrich Nietzsche's madness resulted from brain damage, characteristic of the advanced stages of syphilis.

Evidently, we can confirm that Mia's hair is black (Example 1.16–1). And although we can't do an autopsy on Friedrich, we can confirm by reading that his critics have so speculated (Example 1.16–2). The statement is true, as far as it goes.

**Performative utterances** are not true or false. Instead, if there is something wrong with them, they are "unhappy", while if nothing is wrong they are "happy". The uttering of a performative is part of the doing of a certain kind of action (Austin later refers to them as under the name of illocutionary acts), the performance of which, again, would not normally be described as just "saying" or "describing" something (Austin, 1962).

For example, when Peter says "I promise to do the dishes" in an appropriate context then he thereby is not just saying something, and in particular he is not describing what he is doing. Rather, in making the utterance he performs the promise. Since promising is an illocutionary act, the utterance is thus a performative utterance.

If Peter utters the sentence without the intention of keeping the promise, or if eventually, he ends up not keeping it, then although something is not in order with the utterance, the problem is not that the sentence is false: It is rather "unhappy", or "infelicitous", as Austin (1962) also says in his discussion of so-called felicity conditions. In the absence of any such flaw, on the other hand, the utterance is to be assessed as "happy" or "felicitous" rather than as "true".

**Felicity condition** is a state in which the utterance made has met the appropriate conditions: "(i) a conventional procedure and effect; (ii) the appropriate circumstances; (iii) the correct and complete execution of the procedure by all persons; and (iv) certain thoughts and feelings about the realization of the act on the part of persons involved" (Austin, 1962: 14–15). The notion of "performative action" is fundamental to the analysis of formal and non-formal institutional interactions, because it considers both speakers and hearers co-constructing joint actions in specific socio-cultural contexts. For example, when one is making a promise to another person, he/she has to fulfill the condition that the hearer or promisee has a need for something to be promised, and the speaker or promiser will have the intention to fulfill that need. Thus, the act of promising will be valid to be regarded as a felicitous condition.

### Example 1.17

(1) I do (i.e., take this woman to be my lawful wedded wife). (uttered in the course of the marriage ceremony)

(2) I name this ship the "Queen Elizabeth".

(3) I give and bequeath my watch to my brother. (occurs in a will)

(4) I now pronounce you married. (used in the course of a marriage ceremony)

(5) I order you to go. / "Go"—that's an order.

(6) You are under arrest. (used when arresting someone)

Austin proposed a three-way taxonomy of speech acts: (i) a locutionary act refers to the act of saying something meaningful, that is, the act of uttering a fragment or a sentence in the literal sense (referring and predicating); (ii) an illocutionary act is performed by saying something that has a conventional force such as informing, ordering, warning, complaining, requesting, or refusing; and (iii) a perlocutionary act refers to what we achieve "*by* saying something, such as convincing, persuading, deterring, and even, say, surprising or misleading" (Austin, 1962: 109).

#### 1.2.5.2 Maxims of conversation

In linguistics, the **cooperative principle** describes how people achieve effective conversational communication in common social situations—that is, how listeners and speakers act cooperatively and mutually accept one another to be understood in a particular way.

Linguist Paul Grice (1975: 45) introduced the concept in his pragmatic theory and argued that "... make your contribution such as is required, at the stage at which it occurs, by the accepted purpose or direction of the talk exchange in which you are engaged."

Accordingly, the cooperative principle is divided into Grice's four maxims of conversation, called the **Gricean maxims**—quantity, quality, relation, and manner. The maxim of quantity states that a speaker should be as informative as is required and neither more nor less. The maxim of relevance essentially states that a speaker should stay on the topic, and the maxim of manner states that the speaker should be brief and orderly, and avoid ambiguity. The fourth maxim, the maxim of quality, states that a speaker should not lie or make any unsupported claims.

These four maxims describe specific rational principles observed by people who follow the cooperative principle in pursuit of effective communication. Applying the Gricean maxims is a way to explain the connection between utterances and what is understood from them.

## 1.3  Approaches to language

In general, there are five approaches to the study of language:

- prescriptive vs. descriptive
- synchronic vs. diachronic
- syntagmatic vs. paradigmatic
- competence vs. performance
- linguistics as a science

### 1.3.1  Prescriptive vs. descriptive approaches

The **prescriptive approach** involves laying down rules of a language and stating what is considered right and wrong in the language. It tends to be conservative, and regards changes with suspicion. For example, the rules say that splitting infinitives is wrong in English. Hence, the following sentence of Example 1.18 is a bad sentence because it splits the infinitive "to go".

#### Example 1.18

To boldly go where no one has gone before...

The **descriptive approach** involves describing the way a language works, as observed from actual examples of the language. It describes words and constructions based on their usage. If a word or expression is not found in careful or formal speech or writing, good descriptive practice requires the reporting of this information. For example, it is often the case that some people split infinitives while others don't. Then what kind of people split infinitives? When do they do it? What can be used to split an infinitive? These are the concerns of descriptivism.

The prescriptive approach states that rules must be taught and often involve value judgments. Prescriptivists typically abide by traditional elements that strive to preserve long-standing grammatical rules, word forms, processes or behaviors, even if the rules are outdated. By contrast, descriptivists allow for change and more readily accept changes due to syntax modifications and cultural influences. They believe language is learned or understood rather than taught. For example, you don't need to teach students that their voice goes down at the end of a statement and up at the end of a question.

For example, descriptivists might allow students to use either "slow" or "slowly" to modify a verb because people often use the words interchangeably. On the other hand, prescriptivists would consider the word "slowly" to be the only form that should be used as an adverb.

A common misconception is that descriptivists "have no rules" and have a permissive "anything goes" attitude. In fact, descriptive linguistics is dedicated to describing the rules of language and essentially sees language as rule-governed. Descriptivists seek to find the rules that govern the languages that people speak (e.g., Chinese, French, Korean, etc.). Precriptivists generally seek to impose arbitrary rules that come from outside the language and/or seek to preserve a stage of the language that has been left behind by the evolution of the language itself. For example, language rules say:

- don't use "double negatives" or "double negatives affirm" (Lowth, 1762);

- don't split infinitives;

- don't have postponed prepositions.

In reality, we often hear people say: "I don't want no fish." "He couldn't sleep, not even with a sedative." (He couldn't sleep, even with a sedative.) "No one thought so, not even you." (No one thought so, even you.) "I have tried to consciously stop worrying about it." (I have tried to stop consciously worrying about it. I have consciously tried to stop worrying about it.)

Meanwhile, wh-questions, relative clauses, and exclamations always have postponed prepositions, so does the use of the passive voice sometimes. For example, "What are you looking at?" "She is sought after."

In an ideal world, descriptive and prescriptive approaches to language would follow a harmonious relationship: Linguists would describe the rules of a language, and pedagogues would use these descriptions to design textbooks to teach language learners. Prescriptivism is good for language planning, when the government decides which languages will be taught in schools, and what languages public employees should know.

### 1.3.2   Synchronic vs. diachronic approaches

A **synchronic approach** looks at a language at a moment in time without taking its history into account. Synchronic linguistics aims at describing a language at a specific point of time, usually the present. Synchronic linguistics is often descriptive, analyzing how the parts of a language or grammar work together.

"A synchronic study of language is a comparison of languages or dialects—various spoken differences of the same language—used within some defined spatial region and during the same period of time", wrote Donnelly (1994). Therefore, describing how EFL (English as a foreign language) learners in different parts of the world speak English at present, analyzing grammar, classification, and arrangement of the features of a language are examples of the types of inquiries pertinent to a synchronic study.

A synchronistic approach views a language as if it is static and not changing. Languages are constantly evolving, though so slowly that people don't notice it much while it's happening.

By contrast, a **diachronic approach** considers the development and evolution of a language through history (Ramat et al., 2013). Thus, it studies the historical development of a language throughout different periods of time. This branch of linguistics is called diachronic linguistics. The main concerns of diachronic linguistics are as follows:

- describing and accounting for observed changes in particular languages;
- reconstructing the pre-history of languages and determining their connection, grouping them into language families;
- developing general theories about how and why languages change;
- describing the history of speech communities; and
- studying the history of words (tracing a word back to its origin).

### Example 1.19

(1) Analyze the word order in a sentence in Old English. (a synchronic approach)

(2) Examine how word order changed in a sentence from Old English to Middle English and now to Modern English. (a diachronic approach)

(3) Analyze how historical events affected a language: When the Normans conquered England in 1066, what changes happened to English? (A diachronic look could analyze what new words were adopted, which ones fell out of use, and how long that process took to select words. A synchronic study might look at the language at different points before the Normans or after.)

Though synchronic and diachronic approaches have different foci, they sometimes overlap. In each generation, new words are created, or already existing words change their meanings, and speakers perceive them as neologisms or new words. Meanwhile, old words die out (or become archaisms) and are eventually no longer understood and forgotten. In order to label a word as a neologism or an archaism, one must refer to the diachronic aspect of language, even when one is describing language synchronically.

### 1.3.3　Syntagmatic vs. paradigmatic approaches

Syntagmatic and paradigmatic approaches refer to two kinds of relations between linguistic elements in a language (Saussure, 1983).

A **syntagmatic relation** refers to the sequential characteristic of speech, which can be seen and analyzed at all levels such as phonemes /b/, /ʌ/, /l/, /k/ in the sound sequence /bʌlk/, in the linear order of morphemes "un-, speak, -able" in the word "unspeakable", in the sequence of words "they, are, studying, linguistics" in the sentence "They are studying linguistics". It involves a sequence of signs that together create meaning.

The words in a sentence are all syntagms and together they form a syntagmatic relationship that creates meaning. If the order of syntagms in a sentence is changed, the meaning is changed significantly, as shown in Example 1.20.

### *Example 1.20*

(1) John ate an octopus.

(2) An octopus ate John.

(3) The boy beat the dog.

(4) The dog beat the boy.

Sentences in the Example 1.20 use exactly the same words (syntagms), but express very different meanings because the order (the syntagmatic relationship) of the words in the sentences differs.

A **paradigmatic relation** is a relation between a linguistic element in an utterance and linguistic elements outside the utterance, while still belonging to the same sub-system of the language. A paradigmatic relationship involves signs that can replace each other, usually changing the meaning with the substitution. Take the following sentence as an example: "They are studying linguistics."

The word "they" is clearly related to "you, I, we, he, she", though they are not present in the sentence, which form a sub-system known as the personal pronoun system in English. Thus, the members in this system have a paradigmatic relation. Similarly, the word "are" in the sentence and others "am" and "is" form the "be verb system". Once we choose a member from a system, the other members of the same system cannot co-occur in the same place. Thus, we can't say "They we are studying linguistics." or "They are am studying linguistics."

A syntagmatic relation is about the positioning of elements in a sequence of a language. A paradigmatic relation is about substitution. It describes the vertical dimension of a language. The members that display this kind of relation belong to the same sub-system.

> **Example 1.21** (Crystal, 1971: 166)
>
> We can go tomorrow.     →     syntagmatic relation
>
> She may come soon.
> I will ask next.     →     paradigmatic relation
> You could sleep now.

## 1.3.4  Competence vs. performance

Chomsky (1972, 1986) made a distinction between competence and performance, also termed as I-language (internalized language) and E-language (externalized language).

**Competence** is the knowledge of how a language works. It refers to the native speaker's knowledge of his/her language, its system of rules, and his/her ability to produce and understand the language. **Performance** is the study of the system of rules and the actual use of the language in real-life situations.

Competence is the idealization of performance, which is not affected by such factors as fatigue, the need to eat or other factors. The following statements are true of competence and performance:

- Competence is the speaker's knowledge of the structure of the language; performance is the speaker's use of the language.

- Competence is a set of principles that a speaker masters; performance is what a speaker does.

- Competence is a kind of code; performance is an act of encoding or decoding.

- Competence involves "knowing" the language; performance involves "doing" something with the language.

- It is very difficult to assess competence without assessing performance.

To be more specific,

- Competence is the ability to produce a word (or sentence); performance is actually saying the word (or sentence).

- Competence is what one knows about a word (or sentence); performance is the sound one articulates or makes.

According to Chomsky (1986), competence is an idealized capacity that is thought of as a psychological or mental property or function, and performance is the production of actual utterances. Obviously, one can find out about competence only by studying performance. And there may be a considerable difference between someone's knowledge of their language, and what he/she is actually able to produce, as in the case of children or people suffering from some types of speech disorder.

### 1.3.5   Linguistics as a science

Linguistics is the science of language, and linguists are scientists who apply the scientific method to questions about the nature and function of language. Linguists conduct formal studies of speech sounds, grammatical structures, and meanings of all the world's over 6,000 languages. They also investigate the history of and changes within language families and how language is acquired when we are infants. Linguists examine the relationship between written and spoken language, as well as the underlying neural structures that enable us to use language.

In general, linguistics is a science because:

- it is systematic;

- it consists of a set of true facts that can be proven objectively;

- it studies the natural and physical phenomena of human language;

- it uses the scientific method to determine the nature and principles of language; and

- it uses empirical observations to develop theories of language behavior.

Linguists follow certain procedures to make sure that their conclusions are appropriate:

- Formulate a hypothesis based on the available data;

- Check the validity of the hypothesis against new data;

- Apply the principle of falsification. (It suggests that for a theory to be considered scientific it must be able to be tested and conceivably proven false. For example, the hypothesis that "all swans are white" can be falsified by observing a black swan.)

**Example 1.22**

(1) John loves school. → Does John love school?

(2) John went to school. → Did John go to school?

(3) They want to play. → Do they want to play?

Based on these data, the linguist could produce the hypothesis: To make a question in English, it is necessary to put the auxiliary "do" at the beginning of the sentence in the right tense and person, and change the main verb of the sentence to the bare infinitive form.

However, the linguist encounters the following piece of data:

(1) John is a student. → Is John a student?

(2) They are from the North. → Are they from the North?

What should the linguist do then?

## Tasks

### 1. Explain the following terms.

| | | |
|---|---|---|
| phonology | phonetics | articulatory phonetics |
| phoneme | minimal pair | morpheme |
| bound morpheme | syntax | semantics |
| pragmatics | competence | performance |
| synchronic approach | diachronic approach | syntagmatic approach |
| paradigmatic approach | prescriptive approach | descriptive approach |

### 2. Using the following examples as a model, create five new verbs from nouns. Build a sentence with each of these new verbs to show its meaning.

a. My sister just texted me.

b. You should band-aid the cut.

**3. Decide whether the following forms are possible words of English. Then suppose your job is to invent new names for products, create five new forms that are possible words of English and five that are not.**

sproke     basrn     bmdot     cpoof     fluke

**4. Describe the features of the following phonemes.**

/h/     /p/     /æ/     /g/     /ʊ/

**5. Identify whether the following sets of words are minimal pairs.**

| | | |
|---|---|---|
| A. pear  bare | B. click  brick | C. wet  set |
| D. ban  bad | E. just  lust | F. slam  slang |
| G. bet  bat | H. fit  feet | I. sound  found |
| J. sip  sat | K. reel  real | L. meat  meet |
| M. stem  stream | N. boot  fool | O. back  sack |

**6. Read the following statements and determine whether they are true (√) or false (x).**

1) /dʒ/ is an affricate, velar and voiced consonant. (   )

2) The word "chair" has both referential and denotational meanings. (   )

3) Syntax and meaning are independent of each other. (   )

4) Context must be considered when interpreting the meaning of a sentence. (   )

5) It is a synchronic study to examine how 3rd-year English majors write research articles in English. (   )

6) /bæn/ and /bæd/ are minimal pairs. (   )

7) The sounds /æ/ in /bænd/ and /bæn/ are in complementary distribution. (   )

8) To examine whether and how the image of China reported in America's mainstream media changes, it is better to collect and examine all the reports about China in *New York Times* in recent two years. (   )

9) "The students are playing happily there" is a dependent clause. (   )

10) A prepositional phrase often consists of a preposition and a noun phrase. (   )

**7. Please identify the number of syllables in the following words.**

A. syllable          B. consonant          C. spit

D. beautiful         E. vast               F. expect

**8. Analyze the syllable structure of the following words.**

A. fast              B. swing              C. lie

**9. Discuss the following questions.**

1) Language is creative. Which part of language is the most creative: syntax, sound, morphology, and lexicon? Illustrate your idea with examples.

2) What are the differences between competence and performance?

3) What grammar rules do you remember from school? Make a list, and try to decide whether they are prescriptive or descriptive rules.

4) One might study classical Latin about how Latin was spoken roughly between the 1st century BC and the 1st century AD. One might also study how Latin changed between the 1st century BC and the 1st century AD. Please decide which study is diachronic and which is synchronic.

5) Part of linguistic competence involves the ability to recognize whether novel utterances are acceptable. Consider the following sentences and determine which are possible sentences in English. For each unacceptable one, change the sentence to make it acceptable and compare the two.

a. John's mom left himself with a book to read.

b. The student dirted the table.

c. This is the person who I took a picture.

d. I put on it when I was outside.

e. You was born in 1978.

f. The little baby is eager to talk to.

6) If I want to investigate how students' spoken English improves during a semester, what kind of data shall I collect? Why?

7) Why is linguistics a science?

**10. Projects.**

1) Find some words that have changed in meaning over the years in a dictionary with etymologies and compare their usage over the years.

2) Do you recall any experience in which you were taught a rule that you see now makes no sense? How do you feel about this? Write a short essay documenting your experience and share it with your classmates.

3) A researcher intends to analyze how postgraduate English majors write in English. He thus collects their course papers in English and analyzes their structures and the verbs used for reporting citations. Is this a prescriptive or a descriptive perspective? Why? Synchronic or diachronic? Why?

language

culture

learning

hello

world

## UNIT

## 2

# The study of first language acquisition

# Objectives

In this unit, you will learn

—the three theories on first language acquisition: behaviorism, innatism and interactionism;

—stages of first language acquisition;

—atypical language acquisition.

## 2.1 Theories on first language acquisition

Up to date, there have been three leading theories that claim to account for first language acquisition. The first is behaviorism, identified most closely with psychologist B. F. Skinner, the second is innatism or nativism, most closely identified with linguist N. Chomsky, and there is interactionism, which has many supporters but no central figure.

### 2.1.1 Behaviorism

Behaviorism refers to a psychological approach which emphasizes scientific and objective methods of investigation. This approach is only concerned with observable stimulus-response behaviors, and states that all behaviors are learned through interaction with the environment (McLeod, 2020).

**Assumptions of behaviorism**

The behaviorist movement began in early 1910s when John Watson (1913) wrote an article entitled "Psychology as the behaviorist views it", which set out a number of underlying assumptions regarding methodology and behavioral analysis.

**Assumption 1: All behavior is learned from the environment.**

Behaviorism emphasizes the role of environmental factors in influencing behavior, to the near exclusion of innate or hereditary factors. This essentially amounts to a focus on learning. It emphasizes that we learn new behaviors through classical or operant conditioning (collectively known as "learning theory"). Therefore, when we are born our minds are "tabula rasa" (a blank slate).

**Assumption 2: Psychology should be seen as a science.**

Theories need to be supported by empirical data obtained through careful and controlled observation and measurement of behavior. Watson (1913: 158) stated that "P[p]sychology as a behaviorist views it is a purely objective experimental branch of natural science. Its theoretical goal is ... prediction and control". Behaviorists propose defining variables in terms of observable, measurable events.

**Assumption 3: Behaviorism is primarily concerned with observable behaviors, as opposed to internal events like thinking and emotion.**

Behaviorists prefer not to study cognitions and emotions as only observable (i.e., external) behavior can be objectively and scientifically measured. Hence, internal events such as thinking should be explained through behavioral terms.

**Assumption 4: There is little difference between the learning that takes place in humans and that in other animals.**

There's no fundamental distinction between human and animal behaviors. Thus, research can be carried out on animals as well as humans. As a result, rats and pigeons become the primary source of data for behaviorists, as their environments could be easily controlled.

**Assumption 5: Behavior is the result of stimulus-response.**

All behaviors, no matter how complex, can be reduced to a simple stimulus-response association. As described in Watson (1930: 11), the purpose of psychology is "T[t]o predict, given the stimulus, what reaction will take place; or, given the reaction, state what the situation or stimulus is that has caused the reaction".

In summary, behaviorism considers the mind a blank slate, believes that learning is imitation and habit formation, and thinks that children learn because their actions are "reinforced" with praise or successful communication (Watson, 1913; Skinner, 1966).

This is how most people believe language is learned. The mother says a word and the child repeats it. After sufficient use of the word, the child learns it. Even so, behaviorism cannot answer the question "other spoon" after so much repetition, as presented in the following dialogue.

***Dialogue 2.1*** *(Brown & Attardo, 2008: 195):*

C: Want other one spoon, Daddy.

P: You mean you want the other spoon.

C: Yes, I want other one spoon, please, Daddy.

P: Can you say "the other spoon"?

C: Other ... one ... spoon.

P: Say ... other

C: Other

P: Spoon

C: Spoon

P: Other ... spoon

C: Other spoon. Now give me other one spoon.

Chomsky and other linguists claim that children learn a complete language in about five years and propose the **poverty of stimulus** argument. According to this argument, children are exposed to false starts, incomplete sentences, and odd constructions. Their use of language with others, politeness forms and so on may be corrected, yet their grammar is seldom corrected. The following are famous examples from conversations between the same parent and child (Brown & Attardo, 2008: 195).

*Example 2.1*

C: And Walt Disney comes on Tuesdays.

P: No, he comes on Thursdays.

*Example 2.2*

C: Mommy not a boy, he a girl.

P: That's right!

*Example 2.3 (see Dialogue 2.1)*

Even when parents try to correct, children pay little attention to the corrections. Yet, since children grow up with a more or less perfectly formed language, they are able to speak new sentences they have never heard. Then how is this possible? Imitation definitely can't explain this. In addition, all children tend to produce examples like "I eated fish" and "There is one people" during their linguistic development, while no adult uses these forms. What can explain this? Certainly, behaviorism can't answer these questions.

### 2.1.2   Innatism

Innatism (Nativism) is a philosophical and epistemological doctrine that holds that the mind is born with ideas/knowledge, and that the mind is not a "blank slate" at birth. Innatism asserts that not all knowledge is gained from experience and the senses. It believes that humans are genetically programmed to acquire language. Humans do not have language in their brains, but they have the capacity to acquire it readily and with minimal input, which is termed as a **Language Acquisition Device** (LAD) in the mind (Chomsky, 1972). Presently, it is called **universal grammar** (UG), which refers to the principles that are hardwired in our brains (Brown & Attardo, 2008).

### 2.1.2.1   Universal grammar

UG is "the system of principles, conditions, and rules that are elements or properties of all human languages" (Chomsky, 1975: 29). It "is taken to be a characterization of the child's prelinguistic state" (Chomsky, 1981: 7). Learning an L2 (second language) is mediated by UG and by the L1 (first language).

The universal grammar theory proposes that humans possess innate faculties related to the acquisition of language. Universal grammar consists of a set of atomic grammatical categories and relations that are the building blocks of the particular grammars of all human languages, over which syntactic structures and constraints on those structures are defined. The theory assumes that language consists of a set of abstract principles that characterize the core grammars of all natural languages. In addition to principles that are invariable (i.e., all languages have them), there are parameters that vary across languages. The central idea of principles and parameters is that a person's syntactic knowledge can be modelled with two formal mechanisms:

- A finite set of fundamental **principles** that are common to all languages. For example, a sentence must always have a subject, even if it is not overtly pronounced.

- A finite set of **parameters** that determine syntactic variability amongst languages. For example, a binary parameter that determines whether or not the subject of a sentence must be overtly pronounced.

Take "driving a car" as another example. The principle is that drivers have to keep consistently to one side of the road. The parameters can be different: Right in China and USA, and left in England and Japan.

UG is postulated as an innate language facility that limits the extent to which languages can vary. Principles and parameters do not need to be learned by exposure to language. Exposure to language merely triggers the parameters to adopt the correct setting. It seems that children come to know certain properties of grammar that are obviously not learned from input, as demonstrated in Examples 2.4 and 2.5.

### *Example 2.4*

(1) I want to go.

(2) I wanna go.

(3) Sam wants to go but we don't want to.

(4) Sam wants to go but we don't wanna.

(5) Does she want to look at the pictures?

(6) Does she wanna look at the pictures?

(7) What do you want to see?

(8) What do you wanna see?

Example 2.4 presents the range of possibilities for changing "want to" to "wanna". Yet, in many cases, "want to" can't be replaced by "wanna", as shown in Example 2.5.

### Example 2.5

(9) Who do you want to clean the room?

(10)* Who do you wanna clean the room?

(11) Who do you want to lead the team?

(12)* Who do you wanna lead the team?

White (2003) explains that there are principles of UG involving question formation to account for the distribution of these English forms. Sentence (7) can be represented by something like "You want to see X" and Sentence (9) by something like "You want X to clean the room". The question is about an element (X) that is placed between "want" and "to", which effectively blocks contraction.

However, the input a child receives alone doesn't provide this information. This argument is called the **poverty of stimulus**.

In theory, there are two kinds of evidence available to learners as they make hypotheses about correct and incorrect language forms: positive evidence and negative evidence. **Positive evidence** comes from the speech learners hear/read and thus is composed of a limited set of well-formed utterances of the language being learned. **Negative evidence** is composed of information to a learner that his or her utterance is deviant from the norms of the language being learned. Negative evidence is not frequent for children learning a language. Positive evidence alone cannot delineate the range of possible and impossible sentences. Thus, there must be innate principles that constrain the possibilities of grammar formation.

### 2.1.2.2　Critical period hypothesis (CPH)

The critical period is a crucial piece of evidence for innatists. The critical period hypothesis (CPH) claims that there is an optimal period for language acquisition, ending at puberty. The strongest form of CPH holds that children must acquire their L1 before puberty if they are ever to acquire it at all. A weaker CPH claims that L1 acquisition becomes more difficult after puberty.

The evidence for CPH is a number of feral children raised in the wild, supposedly by wolves, tigers, and other animals, who have found their way to towns. They have been able to learn isolated words and simple structures, but their language development has never approximated that of children of their own age.

### 2.1.2.3  Genie's case (Fuchs, 2007)

Genie's story was revealed on November 4, 1970, in Los Angeles, California. Genie was an adolescent, 13 and a half years old, who did not react to temperature, did not know how to chew, couldn't stand erect or straighten her arms or legs, couldn't run or climb and could only walk with great difficulties. She weighed only 59 pounds and was only 54 inches tall; she was incontinent of feces and urine and she spitted onto anything at hand. Genie didn't vocalize in any way; she was "unsocial, primitive, hardly human". During the years there was little for Genie to listen to. Except for moments of anger when her father swore, Genie did not hear any language and thus received no auditory stimulation of any kind. When she made noise, her father would beat her. Her father, mother, and older brother rarely spoke to her.

Genie's case presented a unique opportunity for researchers. Funded by the National Institute of Mental Health (NIMH), a team of psychologists and language experts began the process of rehabilitating Genie. Given an enriched learning environment, could she overcome her deprived childhood and learn language even though she had missed the critical period? If she could, it would suggest that the critical period hypothesis of language development was wrong. If she could not, it would indicate that the theory was correct.

Starting at a one-year-old level upon her initial assessment, Genie quickly began to add new words to her vocabulary. She started learning single words and eventually began putting two words together, much like young children do. After a year of treatment, she even started putting three words together occasionally. Unfortunately, her language abilities remained stuck at this stage and she appeared unable to apply grammatical rules and use language in a meaningful way.

Genie's case is not simple. She missed the critical period of language learning, was horrifically abused, malnourished and deprived of cognitive stimulation for most of her childhood. As a result, researchers were never able to fully determine if Genie suffered from pre-existing cognitive deficits or cognitive deficits caused by her years of abuse, or if she had been born with some degree of mental retardation.

### 2.1.3  Interactionism

The **interactionist approach** combines ideas from sociology and biology to explain how language develops. According to this theory, children learn language out of a desire to communicate with the world around them. Language emerges from and depends on social interaction. This means that the environment in which we grow up will heavily affect how well and how quickly we learn to talk. For example, infants raised only by their mothers are more likely to learn the word "mama", and less likely to develop "dada".

Interactionism sees interaction as central to first language acquisition. Proponents of interactionism highlight the role of what used to be called "motherese" and is now more often called **child-directed speech** (CDS) or caregiver speech in first language acquisition. CDS includes several modifications designed specifically for babies. CDS is slower, more repetitive and exaggerates the pronunciation of vowels (Dewar & Xu, 2010). There are three main types of modifications in CDS (Mcleod, 1993: 282):

- linguistic modifications, including the simplification of certain speech units and emphasis on various phonemes;
- modifications to attention getting strategies (e.g., visual movements to the face);
- modifications to the interactions between parents and infants.

Experiments suggest that these modifications help babies develop several key abilities such as the ability to discriminate between different speech sounds, the ability to detect the boundaries between words in a stream of speech, and the ability to recognize distinct clauses in a stream of speech (Dewar, 2015).

Generally speaking, CDS is characterized by "a slower rate of speech, a higher pitch, quite varied (singsong) intonation, more pauses, shorter and simpler sentences, frequent repetition, frequent questioning, paraphrase, and a focus on the here and now—what is in front of the caregiver and a child" (Brown & Attardo, 2008: 196). Research shows that infants prefer CDS over normal speech because it is slow, simple and easier to understand (Dewar & Xu, 2010). CDS seems to segment the flow of speech to make it more salient to the child, and the wide pitch seems to function as an attention getter. CDS is an attempt to communicate with the child and is not an effort to teach language. According to Thiessen et al. (2005), CDS is more effective in getting an infant's attention than regular speech. Yet it does help infants learn language as babies pick up words faster with CDS than they would otherwise. It also serves as an important part of the emotional bonding process between the child and parents or caregivers (Shore, 1997).

Innatists consider CDS "degenerate". But research shows that CDS is really much "cleaner" than adult-directed speech: It is actually more grammatical and there are fewer disfluent utterances or run-on sentences (Brown & Attardo, 2008; Sonja, 2010). Moreover, CDS varies with age: Adults tend to increase their production of some features just before children begin to produce them; high-pitched intonation tends to disappear by the time the child is five years old; simplified syntax tends to disappear with age; clarity of speech, such as clear vowels and non-reduced consonants, increases around the time children reach the one-word stage of vocabulary acquisition (Brown & Attardo, 2008).

Fathers and older siblings also play a role in language acquisition. Though probably different from CDS, their speech tends to be shorter with the baby. They are more likely to be less patient with the baby and also ask more for clarification. When the baby's sentences are ill formed, caregivers, fathers and older siblings give at least implicit negative evidence, though they seldom stop and offer a direct correction or "rule" (Chouinard & Clark, 2003; Saxton et al., 2005). All these may help acquisition of the language.

Different cultures have different notions of appropriate CDS (Brown & Attardo, 2008). Some cultures don't simplify their speech for children, but repeat it if there are misunderstandings. Other cultures don't respond to children's initiatives and simply ignore them. Some cultures such as the Javanese and Western Samoans think it worthless to converse with children. Other cultures like the Kaluli and Samoans never repair or recast any incorrect form in the child's speech. In many cultures, a baby's first words are conventionalized. For example, Americans and Chinese would say a baby's first word is "mama" or "dada". Western Samoans would say that a baby's first word is "tae", meaning "shit", because they believe that it is the nature of children to be mischievous and to like to say naughty words (Brown & Attardo, 2008).

Table 2.1 summarizes the features of the three theories on first language acquisition.

**Table 2.1    Features of the three theories on first language acquisition**
(Brown & Attardo, 2008: 198)

|  | **Behaviorism** | **Innatism** | **Interactionism** |
|---|---|---|---|
| Imitation | Essential | Triggers LAD | Part of the process |
| Poverty of stimulus | — | UG | — |
| Critical period | — | LAD shuts off | — |
| CDS | — | Degenerate | Essential |
| Corrections | Essential | Useless | Significant |
| Overextension of rules | — | Rule-governed UG | — |

## 2.2 Stages of first language acquisition

First language acquisition is a universal process regardless of the native language. Babies listen to the sounds around them, begin to imitate them, and eventually start producing words.

Generally speaking, there are six stages of first language acquisition:

- pre-talking stage (0–6 months of age);
- prelinguistic/babbling stage (6–8 months of age);
- holophrasic stage (8–18 months of age);
- two-word production stage (18–24 months of age);
- telegraphic stage (24–30 months of age);
- language stage (30+ months of age).

### 2.2.1  Pre-talking stage

This stage takes place from birth to around six months of age. During this time, infants do not speak, but begin to understand short words and phrases that are central to their needs and interests.

### 2.2.2  Prelinguistic/babbling stage

The babbling phase occurs from around six to eight months old. In this phase, the infant begins to "babble" and makes noises and syllables that are not yet words, like "bbb ..." and "ddd ...". Physically, teeth begin to appear and the muscles in the mouth required for speech begin to develop. Babbling provides babies with the chance to experiment with and control their vocal apparatus—a prerequisite for later speech.

In addition, children from different linguistic communities exhibit significant similarities in their babbling. The tendencies in Table 2.2 are based on data from fifteen different languages, including English, Hindi, Arabic, Japanese, and Thai.

Table 2.2    **Frequently found consonants in babbling** (O'Grady et al., 2011: 371)

| Frequently found consonants | Infrequently found consonants |
| --- | --- |
| p  b  m  t  d  n  k  g  s  h  w  j | f  v |

### 2.2.3  Holophrasic stage

The holophrasic stage is significantly longer, occurring between eight and eighteen months old. During this phase, the infant begins to learn and speak individual words. At the beginning, these words are strongly centered around basic needs and interests, as well as names or identifiers like "mama" and "dada". During this stage, one word like "milk" and "walk" is used to state emotions and needs: one-morpheme, one-unit, basic word stems and single open-class words.

A basic property of these holophrastic/one-word utterances is that they can be used to express the type of meaning that is associated with an entire sentence in adult speech. Hence, a child might use the word "dada" to state "I see Daddy", "milk" to mean "I want milk", and "more" to mean "Give me more water".

As indicated by these words, children seem to choose the most informative word that applies to the situation at hand when producing one-word utterances. For example, a baby who wants milk would say "milk" rather than "want" since "milk" is more informative in the situation. Likewise, a baby who sees a new doll would be more likely to say "doll" than "see", referring to the most striking feature of the situation.

Two phenomena that occur during this stage are under-extensions and over-extensions. An under-extension is the formation of a word-to-concept association that is too narrow, such as "cat" referring to only the family cat. An over-extension, by contrast, is an association that is too broad, such as "cat" referring to all four-legged animals. Mismatches, or idiosyncratic referencing also occurs, resulting in a word being associated with an unrelated concept, such as "cat" referring to a chair (Pinker, 2007). These associations change over time.

Concurrently, children appear to be able to understand many multiword utterances during this period. A study showed that learners in the one-word stage preferred to look at a depiction of Big Bird hugging Cookie Monster, rather than the reverse situation, when they heard the sentence "Big Bird is hugging Cookie Monster" (O'Grady et al., 2011).

### 2.2.4  Two-word production stage

The two-word stage takes place from eighteen to twenty-four months old and introduces simple syntax into the baby's language faculty. Once children have developed single word speech, they begin to pair groups of words together into mini-sentences and phrases with simple semantic relations like "I want" or "give me". Children appear to determine the most important words in a sentence and, almost all of the time, use them in the same order as an adult would (Gleitman & Newport, 1995). Table 2.3 lists some examples of such utterances and their intended meanings.

**Table 2.3    Example utterances of the two-word stage**

| Utterance | Intended meaning |
| --- | --- |
| Mummy hat | "Mummy's hat" |
| baby milk | "baby's milk" |
| water hot | "The water is hot" |
| Daddy busy | "Daddy is busy" |

During this stage, children already demonstrate a three-word comprehension level (Tomasello & Kruger, 1992). The concepts relating to their sentences may therefore be more detailed than the phrases themselves.

### 2.2.5   Telegraphic stage

The telegraphic stage takes place from two to three years old. Over time, children begin to expand their two-word phrases into multi-word/short sentences. They also begin to utilize lexical morphemes to make the words they use fit into the sentence. For example, they understand to use the plural "boys" instead of "boy" when referring to a group of boys. During this stage, their utterances lack grammar and are structured with lexical rather than functional or grammatical morphemes, as shown in Example 2.6.

#### Example 2.6

(1) Baby like milk.

(2) What your name?

(3) I break bottle.

(4) Doll broken.

A common feature of these utterances is the frequent absence of bound morphemes and non-lexical categories. Such utterances are often called telegraphic, because they resemble the clipped style of telegram language.

This stage is characterized by the emergence of quite elaborate types of phrase structure. As the utterances in Example 2.6 show, children are able to form phrases consisting of a head and a complement (e.g., like milk, break bottle), phrases with a modifier (e.g., your, red ), and even full-fledged sentences.

### 2.2.6   Language stage

After the age of three, most children fall into the language stage: Grammar emerges and they create long and complex sentences. In this final stage of language acquisition, children now learn to use functional morphemes to change the meaning of the words they use. Examples include the words "but", "in", "the", and "that".

To conclude, Table 2.4 presents a brief summary of the features of language development at different stages.

**Table 2.4  Normal pattern of speech development** (Schwartz, 1990: 698)

| Age | Achievement |
|---|---|
| 1 to 6 months | coos in response to voice |
| 7 to 9 months | babbling |
| 10 to 11 months | imitation of sounds; says "mama/dada" without meaning |
| 12 months | says "mama/dada" with meaning; often imitates two- and three-syllable words |
| 13 to 15 months | vocabulary of four to seven words in addition to jargon; < 20% of speech understood by strangers |
| 16 to 18 months | vocabulary of 10 words; some echolalia and extensive jargon; 20% to 25% pf speech understood by strangers |
| 19 to 21 months | vocabulary of 20 words; 50% of speech understood by strangers |
| 22 to 24 months | vocabulary of more than 50 words; two-word phrases; dropping out of jargon; 60% to 70% of speech understood by strangers |
| 2 to 2.5 years | vocabulary of 400 words, including names; two- to three-word phrases; use of pronouns; diminishing echolalia; 75% of speech understood by strangers |
| 2.5 to 3 years | use of plurals and past tense; knows age and sex; counts three objects correctly; three to five words per sentence; 80% to 90% of speech understood by strangers |
| 3 to 4 years | three to six words per sentence; asks questions, converses, relates experiences, tells stories; almost all speech understood by strangers |
| 4 to 5 years | six to eight words per sentence; names four colors; counts 10 pennies correctly |

## 2.3  Atypical language development

Not all children reach the same level of language development, yet nothing the children produce is "deviant" or out of the ordinary. Language is often delayed, but follows the same rules of language as typical child language.

This section deals with cases in which typical language development is affected due to trauma or injury. Then a question needs to be asked: How many people are affected by atypical language development or disabilities? The estimate is around 0.5% to 8%–10% (Brown & Attardo, 2008).

### 2.3.1  Hearing impairment

Hearing impairment occurs when there's a problem with or damage to one or more parts of the ear. Hearing impairment varies "along a continuum: It may be very slight and lead only to minor losses of language input (e.g., voiceless consonants), or it may be severe, leading to a total lack of hearing" (Brown & Attardo, 2008: 209). The degree of hearing impairment can vary widely from person to person. Some people have partial hearing loss, meaning that the ear can pick up some sounds; others have complete hearing loss, meaning that the ear cannot hear at all (people with complete hearing loss are considered deaf). With some types of hearing loss, a person may have much more trouble when there is background noise. One or both ears may be affected, and the impairment may be worse in one ear than in the other.

Clearly, if a child has a severe degree of hearing impairment, his or her acquisition of language may be severely affected in that the input can't be processed. According to the National Institute on Deafness and Other Communication Disorders, about 37.5 million American people aged 18 and over are deaf or hard of hearing. That's about 15 out of every 100 people. Another 26 million are regularly exposed to hazardous levels of noise. Hearing loss is also the most common birth anomaly.

Deaf children's articulation is often affected by their lack of input. The production of some sounds may be "off", but the sounds are approximations of typical sounds. Hearing loss from birth up to the age of three has a negative effect on speech/language development, and results in sensory, cognitive, emotional, and academic defects in adulthood by causing delayed development of communicative-linguistic abilities (Shojaei et al., 2016). Children who haven't acquired a first language in the early years might never be completely fluent in any language, and their subsequent development of cognitive activities that depend on a solid first language might be underdeveloped, such as literacy and memory organization (Humphries et al., 2012).

It is the same for syntax. Deaf children have many of the same problems as hearing children, with particular problems with modals, verb auxiliaries and infinitives, and gerunds. Their reading and writing skills are also negatively affected by their limited exposure to language due to their hearing impairment (Brown & Attardo, 2008).

### 2.3.2    Mental retardation

According to the American Association on Mental Retardation, mental retardation (MR) refers to substantial limitations in present functioning. It starts before the age of 18 and is characterized by significantly subaverage intellectual functioning with concurrent limitations in two or more of the following applicable adaptive skill areas: communication, self-care, home living, social skills, community use, self-direction, health and safety, functional academics, leisure, and work.

Levels of MR depend on IQ scores, and a score of 100 is assumed as average, as shown in Table 2.5 (Brown & Attardo, 2008: 209).

**Table 2.5　Different levels of mental retardation**

| IQ | Mental retardation |
|----|--------------------|
| 70–52 | Mild |
| 51–36 | Moderate |
| 35–20 | Severe |
| < 20 | Profound |

Mental retardation is the most common cause of speech delay, accounting for more than 50% of cases (Coplan, 1985). Children with MR demonstrate global language delay and also have delayed auditory comprehension and delayed use of gestures. Generally speaking, the more severe the MR, the slower the acquisition of communicative speech (Alexander & Leung, 1999). Yet their language acquisition follows the same rules as other children. This means that mentally retarded children's language acquisition is not deviant. Mentally retarded children typically match their peers of the same mental age in semantic and pragmatic abilities (Brown & Attardo, 2008). Hence, a child of five but with a mental age of three will show language skills comparable to that of a three-year normal child.

In approximately 30% to 40% of children with MR, the cause is unsure. Known causes of MR include maternal medications, genetic defects, placental insufficiency, intrauterine infection, intoxication, hypoxia, central nervous system trauma, kernicterus, hypothyroidism, meningitis or encephalitis, and metabolic disorders (Leung et al., 1995).

### 2.3.3　Autism

Autism is a neurological developmental disorder, with onset occurring before the child reaches the age of 36 months. It is characterized by delayed and deviant language development, failure to develop the ability to relate to others and ritualistic and compulsive behaviors, including stereotyped repetitive motor activities (Alexander & Leung, 1999). Autistic children seem to be language impaired from the very beginning. Their language development is very slow and includes echolalia, the repetition of another speaker's speech. The speech of some autistic children has an atonic, wooden or sing-song quality.

Autistic children often do not babble or have facial expressions, may avoid looks and may be not responsive. They seem to lack the ability or desire to establish social relations, including with their parents. They generally fail to make eye contact, smile socially, respond to hugs, or use gestures to communicate.

Autism is three to four times more common in boys than in girls. It is almost certainly caused by physiological problems, not by parents' behavior.

### 2.3.4    Stuttering

Stuttering is a speech disorder characterized by repetition of sounds, syllables, or words, prolongation of sounds, and interruptions in speech known as blocks. An individual who stutters knows exactly what he or she would like to say, but has trouble producing a normal flow of speech. These speech disorders may be accompanied by struggle behaviors, such as rapid eye blinks or tremors of the lips. Stuttering can make it difficult to communicate with other people, which often affects a person's quality of life and interpersonal relationships. Stuttering can also negatively influence job performance and opportunities, and treatment can come at a high financial cost.

Research indicates that stuttering is related to the complexity of the speech to be produced: more stuttering in polysyllabic words, in infrequent or unfamiliar words, and in fast speech, less stuttering in word-by-word reading and least in syllable-by-syllable reading (Brown & Attardo, 2008).

Symptoms of stuttering can vary significantly throughout a person's day. In general, speaking in front of a group or talking on the telephone may make a person's stuttering more severe, while singing, reading, or speaking in unison may temporarily reduce stuttering.

Stuttering is sometimes referred to as stammering and more broadly, as disfluent speech. Speech sounds are produced through a series of precisely coordinated muscle movements involving breathing, phonation (voice production), and articulation (movement of the throat, palate, tongue, and lips). Muscle movements are controlled by the brain and monitored through the senses of hearing and touch. The exact mechanisms that cause stuttering are not understood. Stuttering is commonly grouped into two types: developmental and neurogenic.

Stuttering is usually diagnosed by a speech-language pathologist, who is trained to evaluate and treat individuals with voice, speech, and language disorders. The speech-language pathologist will consider a variety of factors, including the child's case history, an analysis of the child's stuttering behavior, an evaluation of the child's speech and language abilities and the impact of stuttering on his or her life.

Currently there is no cure for stuttering. Yet a variety of treatments are available. The nature of the treatment depends on a person's age, communication goals, and other factors. If you or your child stutters, it is important to work with a speech-language pathologist to determine the best treatment options. Many of the current therapies for teens and adults who stutter focus on helping them learn ways to minimize stuttering when they speak, such as speaking more slowly, regulating their breathing, or gradually progressing from single-syllable responses to longer words and more complex sentences. Most of these therapies are also conducive to reducing the anxiety that a person who stutters may experience in some speaking situations.

### 2.3.5　Aphasia

If the brain damage involves the areas of the brain that govern language, it may lead to partial or total loss of language. This is called aphasia. Aphasia can be fluent or nonfluent.

Nonfluent aphasia is also called motor aphasia. The speech of people with nonfluent aphasia is slow, full of hesitation, and often shows errors in pronunciation and omission of words (Brown & Attardo, 2008). One type of nonfluent aphasia is Broca's aphasia, which occurs when there are lesions to a part of the brain called Broca's region. Broca aphasics tend to omit function words and inflectional morphemes. Thus, their speech is also called "telegraphic speech", because it resembles the kind of language used in telegrams.

Fluent aphasics are fluent in producing words, but have difficulty selecting words. A typical case of fluent aphasia is Wernicke's aphasia, in which speakers are fluent, do not hesitate, and generally sound fine, but make very little sense. Often, Wernicke's aphasics tend to produce utterances that are grammatically correct but pragmatically inappropriate, mixed with grammatically incorrect and meaningless fragments (Brown & Attardo, 2008).

Receptive aphasia is another type of aphasia whose primary problem is a deficit in the comprehension of spoken language. Children with receptive aphasia have production difficulties and speech delays. They show normal responses to nonverbal auditory stimuli, but their speech is not only delayed, but also sparse, agrammatic and unclear in articulation. Most children with receptive aphasia gradually acquire a language of their own, which is understood only by those who are familiar with them (Alexander & Leung, 1999).

### 2.3.6　Dyslexia and dysgraphia

Dyslexia is a disorder in reading, while dysgraphia is a disorder in writing. They share symptoms and often occur together. The differences between them are briefly presented in Table 2.6.

**Table 2.6　Differences between dyslexia and dysgraphia**

| | Dyslexia | Dysgraphia |
|---|---|---|
| Definition | An issue that involves difficulty with reading. It can also affect writing, spelling, and speaking. Kids may find it hard to isolate sounds, match sounds to letters or blend sounds into words. | An issue that involves difficulty with the physical act of writing. Kids may also find it hard to organize and express their thoughts and ideas in written form. |

(Continued)

| | Dyslexia | Dysgraphia |
|---|---|---|
| Symptoms | · Struggling with reading<br>· Difficulty sounding out words<br>· Difficulty memorizing sight words<br>· Avoiding reading aloud<br>· Poor spelling and grammar<br>· Not understanding what is being read<br>· Confusing the order of letters<br>· Trouble following a sequence of directions<br>· Difficulty organizing thoughts when speaking | · Illegible handwriting<br>· Slow, labored writing<br>· Mixing print and cursive letters<br>· Spacing letters and words oddly<br>· Poor spelling and grammar<br>· Difficulty gripping a pencil<br>· Incorrect punctuation<br>· Run-on sentences and lack of paragraph breaks<br>· Trouble organizing information when writing |
| Possible effects | · Not meeting expectations can make kids feel inadequate.<br>· Missing verbal jokes, sarcasm and subtle meaning in language can affect kids socially.<br>· Struggling to find the right word or timely answer to a question. | · Messy written work that's full of mistakes may make people believe the kids are lazy or sloppy.<br>· Confusion or frustration at school can make kids anxious.<br>· Avoid taking risks and may have low self-esteem. |
| Strategies | · Specific instruction on identifying sounds, understanding how letters represent sounds in speech and decoding words.<br>· Specialized instruction, either one-on-one or in a small group.<br>· A reading program that focuses on using all the senses to learn. | · Occupational therapy to build fine motor skills and dexterity.<br>· Having kids take a break before proofreading their work.<br>· A checklist for editing their work—spelling, neatness, grammar, syntax, clear progression of ideas, etc.<br>· Using graphic organizers. |

Both dyslexia and dysgraphia can be acquired or developed. Acquired dyslexia and dysgraphia result from brain damage in adulthood. There are three types of acquired dyslexia and dysgraphia: phonological, deep and surface.

### A. Phonological

With phonological dyslexia or dysgraphia, speakers can read or write familiar words but fail to apply the kind of "phonic" rules that unimpaired speakers use to spell new or unfamiliar words (e.g., nonsense words) (Brown & Attardo, 2008).

### B. Deep

In deep dyslexia or dysgraphia, speakers have the same traits as in phonological dyslexia, but with the addition of semantic "errors" (e.g., a patient will read "people" as "person" or write the nonsense syllable "blom" as "flower") (Brown & Attardo, 2008). Errors can be both semantic and phonological/visual levels.

### C. Surface

Patients with surface dyslexia or dysgraphia rely on phonic rules and are unable to read or spell irregular words. (Brown & Attardo, 2008).

Features found in dyslexia include (Brown & Attardo, 2008: 212):

- reading, spelling, and writing below the age level, in spite of no mental retardation and equal or higher IQ than their peers;

- reversal of letters, reversal of ordering, confusion of letters like d/b;

- confusion of left and right, poor directional ability;

- difficulty in putting things in series (like days of the week);

- poor short-term memory.

Dyslexia can manifest itself in many ways. Generally, a child with dyslexia will show a level of performance in a given academic area that is well below average, while having average or above-average intelligence. The child may have aggressive or disruptive behavior, withdraw, cheat, refuse to do homework, and watch a lot of television.

It is easy to misdiagnose dyslexia. The following possible factors need to be ruled out before a diagnosis of dyslexia/dysgraphia can be made (Selikowitz, 1998):

- vision or hearing problems,

- intellectual disability,

- physical disability,

- lack of familiarity with the language of instruction,

- lack of family support,

- poor teaching,

- lack of motivation,

- frequent absenteeism,

- brain damage,

- drugs that impair learning.

Developmental dyslexia and dysgraphia are not acquired and there are no agreed-upon causes for them. Unrecognized developmental dyslexia/dysgraphia may lead to poor performance in school. Yet, research shows no correlation between intelligence or other intellectual factors and developmental dyslexia/dysgraphia (Brown & Attardo, 2008).

# Tasks

## 1. Explain the following terms.

behaviorism       innatism               interactionism       poverty of stimulus

critical period    child-directed speech  babbling             language acquisition device

dyslexia           aphasia                mental retardation   stuttering

dysgraphia         universal grammar      positive evidence    negative evidence

under-extension    over-extension

## 2. Discuss the following questions.

1) What assumptions does behaviorism hold?

2) Is there any evidence against behaviorism's belief of language learning?

3) How is universal grammar related to language acquisition?

4) What is the evidence for and against the critical period hypothesis?

5) What is the role of child-directed speech (CDS)? What features does it have? Is it degenerate?

6) What roles do fathers and old siblings play in a child's acquisition of the language?

7) What is the role of culture in CDS?

8) What are the characteristics of the language in the two-word stage?

9) What are the characteristics of the language in the telegraphic stage?

10) What is the relationship between typical and atypical language development?

11) How is language development affected by mental retardation?

12) How is dyslexia related to language development?

## 3. Projects.

1) Compare and contrast the three theories of first language acquisition. What evidence is there for and against each?

2) If there is a baby sibling at home, keep a diary of one week's language directed to the baby, including the baby's output. How does language (the baby's input and output) fit into the theories described in this unit?

3) Please find out about the CHILDES (Child Language Data Exchange System) project.

language

culture

learning

hello

world

# UNIT 3

# The study of second language acquisition

# Objectives

In this unit, you will learn

—key terms in second language acquisition;

—similarities and differences between first and second language acquisition;

—Krashen's theory of second language acquisition.

## 3.1 Key terms

### 3.1.1 Second language acquisition

**Second language acquisition (SLA)**, or sequential language acquisition, is learning a second language after a first language is already established. It refers to both the study of individuals and groups who learn a language subsequent to learning their first one as young children, and to the process of learning that language. The additional language is referred to as a second language (L2), even though it may actually be the third, fourth, or tenth language to be acquired. It is also commonly called a target language (TL), which refers to any language that is the aim or goal of learning. Generally, children have an easier time learning a second language, but anyone can do it at any age.

### 3.1.2 First language / native language / mother tongue / second language

A **first language** is a person's **mother tongue** or **native language**, while a second language is a language a person learns in order to communicate with speakers of that language. There is no other alternative to a first language. A person who cannot decide his or her first language can choose a second language among other languages.

**Second language** is a term given to a language that a person learns in addition to his or her first language. A second language can be learned in a formal or informal way, such as at school or in a family. It is possible that a person speaks two or more second languages.

### 3.1.3 Formal and informal learning

Formal learning, also called structured learning or synchronous learning, refers to a type of learning program in which the goals and objectives are defined by the training department, instructional designer, and/or instructor. It happens in a training-based organization, workplace, on mobile devices, in classrooms, online over the Internet, and through e-learning portals. It is explicitly designed as education in terms of time, objectives, and resources. It is an intentional learning from the learner's perspective, leading to degrees and certifications.

Informal learning, also called non-formal learning or self-directed learning, is the education that is beyond limitations and goes on outside of a traditional formal learning environment like university, school, or college. It is an education that is seen as a learning which goes on in our daily life or learning projects that we undertake to teach ourselves. It is based on daily life experiences like peer groups, family, media or any other influence in the learner's surrounding. It encompasses a range of activities, including learning cookery skills in a community center, taking part in a project voluntarily, picking up information from TV, and direct interaction with individuals or other informal ways.

To be more specific, formal and informal learning have the following three major differences:

- Formal learning is intentional; informal learning is unexpected.

- Formal learning has a designed and structured course outline; informal learning does not have set guidelines or formulas.

- Formal learning is planned, direct, noncontextual, and formulated; informal learning is spontaneous and happens anytime and anywhere.

### 3.1.4  Bilingualism/Multilingualism

**Multilingualism** is the use of more than one language, either by an individual speaker or by a group of speakers. Multilingual speakers have acquired and maintained at least one language during childhood, the so-called first language (L1). The first language (i.e., the mother tongue) is usually acquired without formal education.

**Bilingualism** is a specific case of multilingualism, in which there is no limit to the number of languages a speaker may dominate. The timing and sequence in which each language is learned leads to distinctions between different kinds of bilingualism. Children acquiring two languages natively from these early years are called simultaneous bilinguals. A person who acquires the second language (L2) after the first one is often referred to as a sequential bilingual.

Additive bilingualism is the phenomenon that occurs when becoming bilingual helps learners to develop positive attitudes toward their native languages and themselves. If learners develop negative attitudes towards their own languages in the process of becoming bilingual, it is called subtractive bilingualism. Successive bilingualism is the process of acquiring an L2 after some competence in the L1 has been established by the time a child is about three years old.

Research shows that people who speak more than one language have been reported to be more adept at language learning compared to monolinguals (Kaushanskaya & Marian, 2009).

As a result, many multilinguals use code-switching in interactions, which involves swapping between languages. In many cases, code-switching is motivated by the wish to express loyalty to more than one cultural group (Trudell, 2005). Code-switching may also function as a strategy when a person is not proficient in a language. For example, code-switching occurs if the person lacks the vocabulary of one of the languages for certain fields, or if the person has not developed proficiency in certain lexical domains, as in the case of immigrant languages.

## 3.2 SLA = First language acquisition?

During the process of learning L1 or L2, learners constantly make and test hypotheses about the language to build an internal representation of the language. For example, after learning a new word, the learner may try using it in different situations to confirm the right use of the word. Hence, the question is: Is second language acquisition the same as or different from first language acquisition? Generally speaking, there are two broad views: the Fundamental Difference Hypothesis (Bley-Vroman, 1989; Schachter, 1988), and the Fundamental Identity Hypothesis (Ellis, 1994).

### 3.2.1 Similarities and differences between second and first language acquisition

There are many similarities between first and second language acquisition, especially in early stages (e.g., the silent period, the use of formulas, simplification, insufficient input, etc.). The following lists some of the similarities.

- The acquisition of syntax, particularly negation and questions, is very similar.

- Morpheme orders are similar but not the same—articles, auxiliaries and the copula are all acquired earlier and the irregular past later in L2.

- Both L1 and L2 learners omit items and substitute nouns for pronouns.

- Universal grammar can influence both L1 and L2 learning.

- There are predictable stages in both L1 and L2 acquisition.

- Making errors is part of the learning process for both L1 and L2.

- Learners use contextual clues, prior knowledge, and interaction to comprehend both L1 and L2.

- Age is an important variable affecting proficiency in both L1 and L2.

- Learners can often comprehend more complex language than they are able to produce in both L1 and L2.

- A learner's proficiency may vary in different situations in both L1 and L2.

- In both first and second language acquisition, learners may overgeneralize vocabulary or rules, using them in contexts broader than those in which they should be used.

- In both first and second language acquisition, learners need comprehensible input and opportunities to learn language in context in order to improve their proficiency.

Meanwhile, differences exist between first and second language acquisition, some of which are listed below:

- Everyone succeeds in L1 but many do not in L2.

- There is little variation in L1 but a lot in L2.

- There is fossilization in L2 but not in L1.

- Instruction and negative evidence (correcting mistakes) seem to help the learning of L2 but not L1.

- Affective factors are very important in L2 but not in L1.

- Universal grammar (UG) and knowledge of L1 serve as a basis for learning L2.

- L1 is "acquired" and L2 is "learned".

- L1 is a natural part of a person's everyday life, but L2 is a new aspect of the person's life.

### 3.2.2    The Fundamental Difference Hypothesis

The Fundamental Difference Hypothesis (FDH), formulated by Bley-Vroman (1989), claims that the nature of the process involved in second language acquisition is radically different from that of first language acquisition. The former process involves a language-specific faculty, the language acquisition device, whereas the latter observes a more general problem-solving skill, also typical of adult learning in various fields other than language. As stated in Bley-Vroman (1989: 50), "... The function of the domain specific acquisition system is filled in adults (though indirectly and imperfectly) by this native language knowledge and by a general abstract problem-solving system. I shall call this proposal the Fundamental Difference Hypothesis."

The FDH believes that children and adults are different in many important ways in language learning: a) the ultimate attainment, b) the type of knowledge these two groups have at the outset of language learning, and c) the motivation and attitudes towards the target language and the target language community. For example, adults can make use of their world knowledge to comprehend L2, while children cannot. Affective factors like motivation and anxiety normally have no impact on child's first language acquisition, but do impact adults' acquisition of a second language.

The FDH argues that adult learners do not have access to universal grammar when learning a second language. What they know of language universals is constructed through their mother tongue. When starting an L2, they know that a language contains an infinite number of sentences, that they are capable of understanding sentences they have never heard before, and that a language has rules of syntax, rules for combining morphemes, limits on possible sounds, and so on (Montrul, 2009). In addition, they make use of their general problem-solving abilities during the process of learning an L2.

The FDH is supported by Montrul (2009) but rejected by Song and Schwartz's (2009) study on Korean "wh"-constructions.

### 3.2.3   The Fundamental Identity Hypothesis

The Fundamental Identity Hypothesis (FIH) claims that the same language-specific mechanism guiding first language acquisition may be involved in second language acquisition as well. Observations show that some, though very few, adult second language learners do achieve native-speaker competence. This might be that the language acquisition device (LAD) is available to second language learners well beyond the critical period.

Ellis (1994) argues that second language acquisition is, in crucial respects, like first language acquisition, and the same theoretical constructs can be invoked to explain both. For example, developmental L2 errors tend to be similar to those committed by L1 learners. L2 morpheme acquisition studies also indicate that the order of acquisition of certain morphemes in L2 is similar to that in L1.

Schwartz's (1997) comparison of acquisition sequences of child and adult second language learners who share a similar language background revealed that "linguistic-specific mechanisms do drive nonnative grammar construction" (15). This finding further supports FIH.

### 3.2.4   Universal grammar and second language acquisition

It is commonly believed that "UG is constant, is distinct from the learner's L1 grammar, constrains the L2 learner's interlanguage grammars" (White, 2003: 60). Generally speaking, there are four different positions on the accessibility of universal grammar to L2 learners: a) no access position, b) indirect access position, c) partial access position, and d) full access position. The last three positions are consistent with the Access to Universal Grammar Hypothesis (AUGH), which argues that the innate language facility is alive in SLA and constrains the grammars of L2 learners as it does the grammars of child L1 learners.

- **No access position:** This position claims that there is no such thing as UG in L2 acquisition.

- **Indirect access position:** This position believes that UG exists in L2 acquisition, but L2 learners only have indirect access to it. The best-known hypothesis of this position is the Fundamental Difference Hypothesis (FDH) (Bley-Vroman, 1989). Bley-Vroman (1989) argues that the mind is modular, and that there exists a language faculty—universal grammar (UG), which is essential for the development of L1. But adult L2 learners do not have direct access to this UG.

- **Partial access position:** This position holds that UG exists, but L2 learners only have partial access to it. It claims that L2 learners have access to principles but not to the full range of parameters (Clahsen & Muysken, 1989; Schachter, 1989).

- **Full access position:** This position believes that L2 learners have full access to UG. It claims that UG is an important causal factor in SLA, though not the only one, and that L1 UG affects the L2 learning process. Researchers adopting the full access position argue that principles not applicable to the L2 learner's L1, but are needed for the L2, will constrain the L2 learner's interlanguage (Farahani et al., 2014). For example, they think that the subjacency principle on wh-movement will constrain a Korean learner's interlanguage grammar, while those adopting the partial access view believe that the subjacency principle would not affect a Korean native speaker learning English, since it is irrelevant to Korean (Song & Schwartz, 2009).

## 3.3 Krashen's theory of second language acquisition

Stephen Krashen is an expert in the field of linguistics, specializing in theories of language acquisition and development. Krashen's (1982, 1985) theory of second language acquisition consists of five main hypotheses:

- the acquisition-learning hypothesis;

- the monitor hypothesis;

- the natural order hypothesis;

- the input hypothesis;

- the affective filter hypothesis.

### 3.3.1 The acquisition-learning hypothesis

The acquisition-learning distinction is the most fundamental of the five hypotheses and the most widely known among linguists and language practitioners. According to Krashen, there are two independent systems of second language performance: the **"acquired" system** and the **"learned" system**.

The "acquired" system or "acquisition" is the product of a subconscious process very similar to the process children undergo when they acquire their first language. It requires meaningful interaction in the target language—natural communication, in which speakers are concentrated not in the form of their utterances, but in the communicative act. The "learned" system or "learning" is the product of formal instruction and it comprises a conscious process which results in conscious knowledge "about" the language, like knowledge of grammar rules.

The following statements describe some of the features of acquisition and learning:

- Acquisition is unconscious; learning is conscious.

- Acquisition leads to judgments based on intuition and "feel"; learning results in knowing about the language and its rules.

- Acquisition is identical to the way children learn languages; Learning leads to the ability to make grammaticality judgments based on rules.

In Krashen's view, learning is less important than acquisition. He claims that learning never becomes acquisition but sometimes there is acquisition without learning. He believes that people acquire language through communicative situations and understanding messages.

### 3.3.2 The monitor hypothesis

The **monitor hypothesis** explains the relationship between acquisition and learning and defines the influence of the latter on the former. It states that consciously learning language (like studying grammar rules or doing vocabulary exercises) can help a person monitor language output, but doesn't improve his/her language ability. The monitoring function is the practical result of the learned grammar. According to Krashen, the acquisition system is the utterance initiator, while the learning system performs the role of the "monitor" or the "editor".

This hypothesis states that acquisition initiates the utterance and is responsible for fluency, and that learning has only one function—serving as an editor. The focus of language learning should be on communication, not on rule learning, so the "monitor" is not very important. The "monitor" acts in a planning, editing and correcting function when three specific conditions are met:

- A focus on form (the speaker must be thinking about correctness);

- The rule must be known;

- The speaker must have time to think.

According to Krashen, the role of the monitor is—or should be—minor, being used only to correct deviations from "normal" speech and to give speech a more "polished" appearance. Krashen also suggests that there is individual variation among language learners with regard to "monitor" use. He classifies learners that use the "monitor" all the time as over-users, those who have not learned or who prefer not to use their conscious knowledge as under-users, and those who use the "monitor" appropriately as optimal users. Generally speaking, extroverts are under-users, while introverts and perfectionists are over-users. Lack of self-confidence is frequently related to the over-use of the "monitor".

Krashen says that children do not use the "monitor", thus they are superior language learners. But other research has shown that while adults learn faster, children are better in the long run, especially in phonology.

### 3.3.3   The natural order hypothesis

The **natural order hypothesis** is the idea that children learning their first language acquire grammatical structures in a pre-determined, natural order, and that some are acquired earlier than others. This idea has been extended in Krashen's theory of language acquisition to account for second language acquisition, which is based on morpheme studies (Dulay & Burt, 1974; Fathman, 1975). The acquisition of grammatical structures follows a "natural order", which is:

- pronoun case *he/him*

- articles

- copula *be*

- progressive *-ing*

- plural *-s*

- aux *be* + v + *-ing*

- regular past

- irregular past

- plural *-es*

- possessive *'s*

- third person singular *-s*

This hypothesis states that there are predictable stages, that language acquisition follows predictable patterns, and that certain grammatical structures will almost always be acquired before others, regardless of age. For a given language, some grammatical structures tend to be acquired early while others late. This order seems to be independent of learners' age, L1 background, and conditions of exposure. Also, language instruction does not change this natural order.

It is worth noting that the instructional order is not the same as the natural order. Krashen points out that the implication of the natural order hypothesis is not that a language program syllabus should be based on the order found in the studies. In fact, he rejects grammatical sequencing when the goal is language acquisition.

This hypothesis also implies that teachers should get out of the way. But teachers can observe and supervise if a certain student falls out of the order.

### 3.3.4 The input hypothesis

The **input hypothesis** attempts to explain how the learner acquires a second language, i.e. how second language acquisition takes place. The input hypothesis is only concerned with "acquisition", not "learning". According to this hypothesis, the learner improves and progresses along the "natural order" when he/she receives second language "input" that is one step beyond his/her current stage of linguistic competence. For example, if a learner is at a stage "i", then acquisition takes place when he/she is exposed to "comprehensible input" that belongs to level "i + 1".

Comprehensible input in a language refers to the language that one can understand. Language inputs include things one hears (like podcasts, the radio, conversations, and so on), as well as things one reads (like books, articles, English blog posts, etc.). Krashen is careful to emphasize that one can't just read or listen to anything to improve one's language. One has to read or listen to content that he or she can understand. Language acquisition occurs most effectively when the input is just slightly more advanced than one's own level.

Since not all learners are at the same level of linguistic competence simultaneously, Krashen (1982) suggests that natural communicative input is the key to designing a syllabus. This ensures that each learner will receive some "i + 1" input appropriate for his/her current stage of linguistic competence.

This hypothesis is based on how children learn an L1. Children remain silent, and take in what they hear. Then they babble and actively try out speech. This hypothesis suggests that humans acquire language in one way: by understanding messages received at a level just above their current competence, namely comprehensible input at "*i* (the learner's current language level) + 1 (the next level of language acquisition/the language that is slightly more advanced than the current level)".

Research has shown that learners with more exposure to a second language are more proficient in the language, and that adults who read more have larger vocabulary (Hafiz & Tudor, 1989; Krashen, 1989). Language teaching methods and immersion programs which rely on comprehensible input, like the natural approach and total physical response have led to (very) successful outcomes (Krashen & Terrell, 1983). These findings demonstrate that learning can and often does occur simply from language input—reading and listening. This suggests that it is exposure to language rather than instruction that leads to better linguistic development. Namely, if input is understood, language ability increases accordingly, and the necessary grammar is automatically provided.

Krashen (2011) further suggests that input should not only be comprehensible but also compelling. As Krashen says, "... to make sure that language acquirers pay attention to the input, it should be interesting. But interest may be not enough for optimal language acquisition. It may be the case that input needs to be not just interesting but compelling." Krashen argues that if the learner isn't interested in the input, they won't pay attention to it.

The input hypothesis stresses the importance of reading and listening. Then, how about output? Aren't speaking and writing important as well? In fact, Krashen denies the important role of output. On the contrary, Swain (1985) proposes the comprehensible output hypothesis, which argues that some language learning occurs when a learner produces output and notices a gap in their language ability. Based on the gap, the learner then changes his/her output approach, and thus develops his/her language ability. Swain (Swain & Lapkin, 1995) claims that the output hypothesis can explain language acquisition to a certain degree, though not all.

Krashen (1998) disagrees on the output hypothesis for the following reasons:

a) Output is relatively rare in language learning. Language learners do not speak and write nearly as much as they listen or read.

b) Some individuals achieve significant language acquisition without much output.

c) There is a lack of direct evidence supporting the output hypothesis.

### 3.3.5 The affective filter hypothesis

The **affective filter hypothesis** claims that a number of "affective variables" play an important though not causal role in second language acquisition. These variables include motivation, self-confidence, emotions, anxiety, personality traits, and so on. Learners with high motivation, self confidence, good self-image, low anxiety and extroversion are better equipped for success in second language acquisition. Low motivation, low self-esteem, anxiety, introversion and inhibition can raise the affective filter and form a "mental block" that prevents comprehensible input from being used for acquisition. In other words, when the filter is "up", it impedes language acquisition. On the other hand, positive affect is necessary, but not sufficient on its own, for acquisition to occur.

According to this hypothesis, the affective filter determines which language dialects people will adopt, when acquisition attempts will stop, how fast a learner will acquire an L2, and so on. Krashen believes that children have no affective filter and therefore learn quickly.

### 3.3.6    The role of grammar in Krashen's view

According to Krashen, the study of language structure can have general educational advantages and values that high schools and colleges may want to incorporate in their language programs. However, examining irregularities, formulating rules and teaching complex facts about the target language is not language teaching, but rather "language appreciation" or linguistics.

The only instance in which the teaching of grammar can lead to language acquisition (and proficiency) is when students are interested in the subject and the target language is used as the medium of instruction. Very often, when this occurs, both teachers and students are convinced that the study of formal grammar is essential for second language acquisition, and the teacher is skilled enough to present explanations in the target language so that students can understand. In other words, the teacher's talk meets the requirements for comprehensible input and perhaps, with student participation, the classroom becomes an environment conducive to acquisition. Also, the filter is low in regard to the language of explanation, as the students' conscious efforts are usually on the subject matter, on what is being talked about, and not on the medium.

## Tasks

**1. Explain the following terms.**

| | | |
|---|---|---|
| second language acquisition | first language | second language |
| bilingualism | multilingualism | additive bilingualism |
| informal learning | formal learning | partial access position |
| full access position | acquisition-learning hypothesis | monitor hypothesis |
| input hypothesis | natural order hypothesis | affective hypothesis |

**2. Read the following statements and decide whether they are true (√) or false (x).**

1) A second language can be any language that is learned after the mother tongue. (   )

2) When informal learning is intentional, it leads to success. (   )

3) A multilingual learner is often better at language learning. (   )

4) Code-switching occurs when a bilingual learner is not proficient in one language. (   )

5) Morpheme orders are the same in first and second language acquisition. (   )

6) Generally speaking, learners overgeneralize rules in both first and second language acquisition. (   )

7) The Fundamental Difference Hypothesis states that second language acquisition is partially different from first language acquisition. (   )

8) The Fundamental Identity Hypothesis is supported by the finding that some adult second language learners achieve native-speaker competence in an L2. (   )

**3. Discuss the following questions.**

1) Some educators compare formal learning to taking a bus and informal learning to riding a bike. Do you agree? Why or why not?

2) What does the input hypothesis mean to teaching a second language?

3) Do you use "monitor" when learning English? When and how? Does it affect your learning of English? How?

4) Do you code-switch between Chinese and English? Why and when?

5) Do you agree with the acquisition-learning hypothesis? Why or why not?

6) How does motivation affect your learning of English? Please illustrate your point with examples.

7) What implications does the natural order hypothesis have for teaching a second language?

8) List 3–5 strengths/weaknesses of Krashen's theory of second language acquisition.

**4. Projects.**

1) Observe a baby learning its first language and an adult beginning to learn a second language. Keep a log of their daily use of the languages for one month. Analyze the data and compare the results. Use the theories you have learned to explain your findings.

2) Design a study to test the monitor hypothesis: a) use of monitor, and b) effects of monitor on college students' English speaking.

language

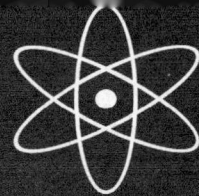

culture

learning

hello

world

**UNIT**

**4**

Interlanguage

# ⤊ Objectives

In this unit, you will learn

—terms like interlanguage and fossilization;

—language transfer and types of language transfer;

—different types of knowledge;

—psycholinguistic constructs involved in language acquisition.

## (4.1) Key terms

### 4.1.1　Interlanguage

The term "interlanguage" was proposed by Larry Selinker (1972), an American professor of applied linguistics. According to Selinker, the process of learning a second language is characteristically non-linear and fragmentary, marked by a mixed landscape of rapid progression in certain areas and slow movement, incubation, or even permanent stagnation in other areas. Such a process results in a linguistic system known as "interlanguage".

Interlanguage is the type of language or linguistic system used by second- and foreign-language learners who are in the process of learning a target language (TL). It is metaphorically a halfway house between the L1 and the TL, hence "inter". The L1 is purportedly the source language that provides the initial building materials to be gradually blended with materials taken from the TL, resulting in new forms that are neither in the L1 nor in the TL.

Interlanguage is affected by the learner's native language, as the learner uses his or her native language knowledge to understand and organize the second language or to compensate for existing competency gaps. It is entirely different from both the learner's L1 and L2. It has its own system of rules but contains ungrammatical sentences and elements.

Interlanguage is dynamic and permeable. It serves as a bridge between L1 and L2 when learners lack knowledge and fine mastery of the rules. Yet learners progress over time and their interlanguage reflects that progress. For example, at the very beginning, a learner may say: "I no eat", which later becomes "I don't eat". The process of constant extension and revision of rules reflects the tendency of interlanguage to change. Interlanguage's rules are changing: They're altered, deleted, or added. Concurrently, a learner's performance changes in different situations. Learners may apply the same rule differently in separate contexts or domains. Accuracy and fluency vary across occasions as learners have alternative rules for the same function. For example, a learner may say: "I went to the supermarket at 7:00 pm" in class when he/she is focusing on grammar, but say "I goes to supermarket at 7:00" in a spontaneous conversation.

Interlanguage is systematic. Although different learners have different interlanguage, they all have their own rules within their variations. The rules may not be consistent with the actual rules, but they are systematic. For example, a learner may say: "I walked to the park, buyed a flower and eated a cake."

According to Brown (1987), there are four stages of interlanguage development, as shown in Table 4.1.

**Table 4.1   Four stages of interlanguage development**

| Stage | Features |
|---|---|
| 1. Random errors or pre-systematic stage | a) The learner is hardly aware of the systematicity attached to the L2 system. <br> b) The learner tends to experiment with the language and produces errors at random. |
| 2. Emergent stage | a) The learner is more aware of the rules of the L2 system and is able to apply them in a relatively successful manner. <br> b) The learner continues to make errors and cannot correct them on his/her own. <br> c) The learner is in his/her comfort zone and avoids using certain structures. <br> d) The phenomenon of backsliding (the variational reappearance of interlanguage features that appear to have been eliminated) is likely to occur. |
| 3. Systematic stage | a) The learner shows greater consistency in producing the L2. <br> b) Output approximates TL norms, even though the rules are not all well-formed. <br> c) The learner is capable of self-correction when prompted to do so. |
| 4. Stabilization or post-systematic stage | a) The learner produces few instances of incorrect language, and is able to self-correct. <br> b) The learner's linguistic system is far from native speaker competence. <br> c) The stabilized language is more likely to "get stuck" than to develop (i.e., the learning process begins to resemble a "plateau", or pre-stage of fossilization). |

### 4.1.2  Fossilization

The term "fossilization" was also coined by Selinker (1972) to refer to the process in the learning of a second language in which the student has more and more difficulties in developing his/her fluency in the language, until eventually, the student is unable to learn any more. The language, for all intents and purposes, is set in stone in the learner's mind at this last point. Some potential for learning small, superficial aspects of the language might still exist, such as vocabulary, but conceptual understanding of the material will not develop any further. Fossilization, thus, is a sort of stagnation in second language acquisition that cannot be overcome.

Fossilization refers to the process in which incorrect language becomes habitual and cannot easily be corrected. For example, many advanced learners whose L1 is Chinese do not distinguish between "he" and "she". This could be a fossilized error.

Errors in general should be corrected in time, but a fossilized error may never be corrected unless the learner sees a reason to do so. Teachers can help learners notice their fossilized errors by recording their speaking, or by asking them to keep a record of written errors as part of a language portfolio.

Fossilization occurs due to various reasons, including negative language transfer (Selinker, 1972). And it is hard to determine when certain users may begin to fossilize. It varies widely with the individual and the environment in which the language is learned. Yet, it often occurs in an inadequate learning environment, although it may occur despite complete immersion in a foreign language environment for decades (e.g., among immigrants).

Fossilization in second language acquisition can also be classified into temporary fossilization and permanent fossilization. As the terms suggest, the former is unstable and changeable, while the latter is in a state of stabilization.

## 4.2 Language transfer

Language transfer is the application of linguistic features from one language to another in speaking or writing by a bilingual or multilingual speaker. Language transfer may occur across languages in the acquisition of a simultaneous bilingual, from a mature speaker's first language (L1) to a second (L2) or third (L3) language they are acquiring, or from an L2 back to the L1 (Chang & Mishler, 2012). Language transfer is also known as language interference/ L1 interference, linguistic interference and cross-linguistic influence. So a more balanced definition of language transfer is that it refers to the influence of a person's knowledge of one language on that person's knowledge or use of another language (Jarvis & Pavlenko, 2008). Linguists agree that language transfer is used by language learners especially when they are unsure about which structure to use in the L2.

### 4.2.1　Types of language transfer

Because languages are different, language transfer can have a positive or negative impact depending on whether the native and second languages share the specific structure used by the learner. Generally speaking, transfer can be positive, negative, conscious and unconscious.

#### 4.2.1.1 Positive transfer

When the relevant unit or structure of both languages is the same, linguistic interference can result in correct language production called positive transfer (Nitschke et al., 2010; Shatz, 2016).

Generally speaking, the more similar the two languages are and the more the learner is aware of the relation between them, the more positive transfer will occur. For example, since the basic sentence structure of both Chinese and English is "subject + verb", it is easy for a Chinese learner of English to positively transfer this structure into English when producing utterances in English.

#### 4.2.1.2 Negative transfer

Negative transfer occurs when speakers and writers transfer items and structures that are not the same in both languages. Within the theory of contrastive analysis which advocates a systematic study of a pair of languages with a view to identifying their structural differences and similarities, the greater the differences between the two languages, the more negative transfer can be expected (Porter & Duncan, 1953). For example, in English, a preposition is used before a day of the week: "I'm going to town on Thursday". In Chinese, no preposition is used: "wo zhousi qu chengli". Beginning Chinese learners of English may produce a transfer error and say "I'm going to town Thursday". English learners of Chinese may overuse or misuse articles in Chinese because there are no articles in Chinese. For example, the Chinese utterance "wo yao mai shu—I want buy book" corresponds to "I want to buy a book (or books)" in English.

### 4.2.2 Explanations for language transfer

Of various approaches to explain language transfer, the most recognized are the Contrastive Analysis Hypothesis and the Markedness Differential Hypothesis.

#### 4.2.2.1 Contrastive Analysis Hypothesis

Lado (1957) proposes the Contrastive Analysis Hypothesis (CAH), which is concerned with the comparison of two or more languages to determine the differences or similarities between them. It implies a belief in language universals: If there are no common features, there may be no basis for comparison. Lado (1957) believes that the degree of difference between two languages correlates with the degree of difficulty. And the difficulty manifests itself in errors: The greater the difficulty, the more frequent the errors. If two languages are similar or identical, positive transfer from the native language may promote SLA; if they are different, negative transfer from the native language may hinder the acquisition of the target language. Using structuralist linguistic methods, Lado (1957) sets out procedures for the comparison of phonology, grammar, and vocabulary, and discusses ways in which such analyses might be relevant to syllabus and materials design, methodology, and testing.

Generally speaking, the CAH holds that L1–L2 differences are both necessary and sufficient to explain the difficulty that occurs in L2 learning. Under this view, all difficulty in L2 acquisition should occur only in areas of difference between the NL (native language) and TL (target language), and thus L1 interference is paramount as an explanatory principle in L2 acquisition theory.

### 4.2.2.2    Markedness Differential Hypothesis (MDH)

Eckman's (1977) Markedness Differential Hypothesis (MDH) argues that the areas of difficulty that a second language learner will have can be predicted on the basis of the comparison of the native language and the target language.

The MDH makes crucial use of the concept markedness, a relational term that has been viewed in different ways by different approaches. According to the MDH, markedness is defined as a phenomenon: A is more marked in a language than B if the presence of A in the language implies the presence of B, but the presence of B does not imply the presence of A. Thus, markedness refers to the relative frequency or generality of a given structure across the world's languages. Crystal (1992) defines "markedness" as an analytic principle in linguistics, whereby pairs of linguistic features, seen as oppositions, are given values of positive (marked) or negative/neutral (unmarked). In its most general sense, this distinction relates simply to the presence or absence of a particular characteristic. For example, a plural noun in English might be said to be "marked for number" (a plural ending having been added to the unmarked singular form). It can also be said that "marked" refers to the way words are changed or added to give a special meaning, and the unmarked choice is just the normal meaning. For example, for English verbs, the present tense (e.g., "walk") is unmarked and the past tense is marked (e.g., "walked").

Using these markedness relations, the MDH makes three claims:

a) The areas of the TL that differ from the NL and are more marked than the NL will be difficult.

b) The relative degree of difficulty of the areas of the TL that are more marked than the NL will correspond to the relative degree of markedness.

c) The areas of the TL that are different from the NL, but are not more marked than the NL will not be difficult.

As discussed, the goal of the MDH is the same as that of the CAH: to explain language transfer and difficulty in L2 acquisition. The MDH, however, is capable of accounting for some things that the CAH cannot account for: (a) Why some NL–TL differences do not cause difficulty, and (b) why some differences are associated with degrees of difficulty and others are not.

## 4.3 Input, interaction and output

### 4.3.1 Input

According to the **Input Hypothesis** (Krashen, 1982), **input** is very important in that it provides language-specific information for a learner to successfully acquire a second language. Ellis (2003) proposes two aspects of input that influence L2 acquisition: input frequency and comprehensible input. Input that is accurate and intensive leads to better L2 acquisition, while limited input might cause unsatisfactory L2 acquisition. Meanwhile, input must be both comprehensible and at a stage slightly beyond the learner's previously acquired linguistic competence (i+1) in order to be acquired (Krashen, 1982). Namely, if input is understood, the necessary grammar is automatically provided; if input is not comprehensible, it cannot serve acquisition at all.

Generally speaking, there are two major types of evidence in input: positive evidence and negative evidence.

#### 4.3.1.1 Positive evidence

Positive evidence refers to the input that basically comprises the set of well-formed sentences to which learners are exposed. These utterances are available from the spoken language and/or from the written language. This is the most direct means by which learners can form linguistic hypotheses.

#### 4.3.1.2 Negative evidence

In language acquisition, negative evidence refers to the type of information that is provided to learners concerning the incorrectness of an utterance. This can take the form of explicit/direct or implicit/indirect information, as shown in Examples 4.1 and 4.2. Explicit evidence is an overt correction. Implicit evidence can result in a communication breakdown or a recast.

#### Example 4.1

> NNS (non-native speaker): I goed to school.
>
> NS (native speaker): No, say, I went to school.

#### Example 4.2 (Mackey, Gass & McDonough, 2000)

> NNS: There's a basen of flowers on the bookshelf.
>
> NS: A basin?
>
> NNS: Base.

> NS: A base?
>
> NNS: A base.
>
> NS: Oh, a vase.
>
> NNS: Vase.

Negative evidence does not show what is grammatical; that is the role of positive evidence. In theory, negative evidence would help eliminate ungrammatical constructions by revealing what is not grammatical. Direct negative evidence refers to comments made by an adult language instructor in response to a learner's ungrammatical utterance. Direct negative evidence in language acquisition consists of utterances that indicate whether a construction in a language is ungrammatical (Lust, 2006). Direct negative evidence differs from indirect negative evidence in that it is explicitly presented to a language learner (e.g., a child might be corrected by a parent).

Indirect negative evidence refers to the absence of ungrammatical sentences in the language that the language learner is exposed to. Indirect negative evidence is used to identify ungrammatical constructions in a language by noticing the absence of such constructions (Lust, 2006) (see Example 4.3). However, in many cases, negative evidence may not help a learner to learn a particular rule of the L2.

**Example 4.3**

> Student: My sister holded the doll and I touched it.
>
> Teacher: Did you say your sister held the doll?
>
> Student: Yes.
>
> Teacher: What did you say she did?
>
> Student: She holded the doll.
>
> Teacher: Did you say she held the doll?
>
> Student: Yes, she holded the doll and I touched it.

As revealed in Example 4.3, the student is seemingly unable to detect the differences between his ungrammatical sentences and the teacher's grammatical sentences. Therefore, he cannot use negative evidence to learn that an aspect of grammar, such as the irregular past tense "holded" in English, is ungrammatical. This example also shows that there must be something other than explicit feedback which drives second language learners to arrive at a correct grammar.

Several types of implicit direct negative evidence are often used to respond to learners' ungrammatical utterances: repetition, recast, expansion, and request for clarification.

Repetitions occur when a teacher repeats a learner's utterance word for word, whereas recasts occur when a teacher repeats a learner's utterance while correcting the ungrammatical parts of the sentence. Expansions are similar to recasts in that they are potentially corrective utterances, but in expansions, a teacher also extends the learner's original utterance. Requests for clarification occur when a teacher asks a question that can prompt a learner to correct an ungrammatical sentence he/she previously said.

### 4.3.2    Interaction

#### 4.3.2.1    The Interaction Hypothesis

Interaction cannot be separated from input and output as interaction acts as a mediator or tool between the two. Given that interaction may occur at the same time as input, the interaction process appears to be the practical tool for learners to contextualize the input they get. The importance of interaction in second language acquisition is best illustrated in the **Interaction Hypothesis** proposed by Long (1996), which integrates the **Input Hypothesis** and the **Output Hypothesis** of second language acquisition. The Input Hypothesis states that a language learner needs to be provided with input in the form of reading, listening to conversations, and grammar and vocabulary instruction. The Output Hypothesis stresses the importance of practicing and speaking to retain and remember the language. It states that one of the most effective methods of learning a new language is through personal and direct interaction. Interaction is not only a means for a learner to study the language, but also a way for the learner to practice what he/she has learned. The main ideas of the Interaction Hypothesis are:

a) comprehensible input is a prerequisite for second language acquisition;

b) input is made comprehensible to the learner via negotiations of meaning in conversations;

c) participation in tasks that require communication and in which participants share a symmetrical role relationship promotes more opportunities for meaning negotiation.

Interactions provide a context for learners to receive feedback on the correctness or incorrectness of their language use. Among the various types of interactions, conversation is probably the one most emphasized in the Interaction Hypothesis. Negotiation of meaning in conversations provides corrective feedback and encourages the process of noticing and attention, which is beneficial for second language acquisition (Ellis, 1991). What is intended is that through focused negotiation work, the learner's attentional resources may be directed to: a) a particular discrepancy between what he or she "knows" about the second language and what is reality vis-à-vis the target language, or b ) an area of the second language about which the learner has little or no information. Learning may take place "during" the interaction, or negotiation may be an initial step in learning (Gass, 1997).

**Example 4.4** (Mackey, 1999)

> NS: There's a pair of reading glasses above the plant.
>
> NNS: A what?
>
> NS: Glasses, reading glasses to see the newspaper.
>
> NNS: Glassi?
>
> NS: You wear them to see with, if you can't see. Reading glasses.
>
> NNS: Ahh ahh glasses to read, you say reading glasses.
>
> NS: Yeah.

In the penultimate line, the NNS acknowledges the fact that the new word "reading glasses" emerged from the interaction and, in particular, as a consequence of the negotiation work.

The Interaction Hypothesis is one of many potential approaches to language learning pedagogy and has a lot of benefits in application. Interactivity in the classroom is not only a good idea for promoting language acquisition. It also promotes a healthy, collaborative, and student-centered culture in which students look to each other, in addition to their instructor, for assistance.

### 4.3.2.2 Foreigner talk

It has been observed that native speakers (NSs) adjust their speech in conversations with non-native speakers (NNSs) in multiple ways. This modified register was termed "foreigner talk" by Stanford University professor Charles A. Ferguson (1975), one of the founders of sociolinguistics. He asserts that foreigner talk is the reduced and simplified version of a language that native speakers use to address other speakers for whom the language is not a native one, especially speakers who do not know the language at all.

Foreigner talk is close to child-directed speech and promotes learning as well as communication with L2 learners. Long (1996) states that foreigner talk posits interaction between NNSs and NSs, creating a naturalistic second language acquisition environment where NNSs learn through negotiating meaning and paying attention to the gaps in their target language knowledge. According to Ellis (1991), there are commonly two broad types of foreigner talk: ungrammatical and grammatical.

Ungrammatical foreigner talk is socially marked, and is characterized by the deletion of certain grammatical features such as copula be, modal verbs (e.g., "can" and "must") and articles, the use of the base form of the verb in place of the past tense form, and the use of special constructions such as "no + verb" (e.g., "He no go"). There is no convincing evidence that learners' errors derive from the language they are exposed to.

Grammatical foreigner talk is the norm. Various types of modification of baseline talk (i.e., the kind of talk native speakers address to other native speakers) can be identified. Studies show that foreigner talk is largely grammatical, simplified (Speech is slower, sentences are shorter, syntax is less complex, and vocabulary is easier), regularized (Speakers use full forms instead of contractions, have fewer false starts, and put the topic at the beginning of the sentence to make comprehension easier. Speakers also use superordinate vocabulary instead of subordinate vocabulary), and elaborated (Synonyms and paragraphs are used extensively). In addition, other features of foreigner talk are: Speech is about the here and now; conversations tend to follow the pattern of question/answer; new topics are much more likely to be initiated by questions; there are many more comprehension checks.

### Example 4.5

NNS: How have rising prices changed your eating habits?

NS: Well, we don't eat as much beef as we used to. We eat more chicken, and uh, pork and uh, fish, things like that.

NNS: Pardon me?

NS: We don't eat as much beef as we used to. We eat more chicken and uh, uh pork and fish... We don't eat beef very often now. We don't have steak like we used to.

NNS: Oh, okay.

### Example 4.6

NS: What classes do you have at 10 o'clock?

NNS: Sorry? 10 clock?

NS: What classes at 10 o'clock?

NNS: 10 o'clock, classes, uh... History.

The functions of foreigner talk can be easily seen in Example 4.5, where the NS repeated and elaborated on the statement after the NNS indicated a lack of understanding, in order to provide the NNS with a comprehensible input. Likewise, the NS repeated in Example 4.6, but in a more simplified form. In addition, the NS provided the NNS with the clue that "10 clock" should be supposedly said as "10 o'clock". Hence, the NNS comprehended what was being asked.

### 4.3.2.3 Interlanguage talk

Interlanguage talk refers to the interaction between a nonnative speaker and a nonnative speaker (NNS/NNS). It is characterized by a lot of negotiation of meaning, such as "Right? No, left. OK, left".

Interlanguage talk is often practiced in second language classrooms because pair work and group discussion lead to a lot of negotiation of meaning, which helps with acquisition. What is not so good about interlanguage talk is that it is less grammatical than foreigner talk, and that ungrammatical input may lead to a pidginized variety of the target language. All these are illustrated in Examples 4.7–4.11, where interlocutors use various strategies like confirmation checks, comprehension checks, clarification requests and reformulations to check and clarify meanings for communication.

*Example 4.7 Confirmation check* (Mackey & Philp, 1998)

> NNS: What are they (.) what do they do your picture?
>
> NS: What are they doing in my picture?
>
> NS: There's just a couple more things.
>
> NNS: A sorry? Couple?

*Example 4.8 Comprehension check* (Varonis & Gass, 1985)

> NNS1: And your family have some ingress.
>
> NNS2: Yes ah, OK, OK.
>
> NNS1: More or less OK?

*Example 4.9 Clarification request*

> NNS1: Can I have the—?
>
> NNS2: What?
>
> NNS1: The v[eiz].
>
> NNS2: The v[eiz]?
>
> NNS1: Yes that v[eiz].
>
> NNS2: The v[a:z]?
>
> NNS1: Yes the v[a:z].

*Example 4.10 Reformulations or "choice"*

> NNS1: What do you want? Ask for way?

NNS2: Uh hotel night?

NNS1: What do you want? Ask for way? or how much is hotel night?

***Example 4.11 Other modifications include topic-focused questions***

NNS1: When do you go to Beijing? You said you saw Tiananmen Square, right?

NNS2: Yeah.

NNS1: When?

### 4.3.3 Output

Input refers to the processible language the learners are exposed to while listening or reading (i.e., the receptive skills). Output is the language learners produce, either in speaking or writing (i.e., the productive skills). It is the result of instant interaction, which can be assumed as the "activation of previous knowledge" of the second language. The Output Hypothesis (Swain, 1985) says that output is as important as input in second language acquisition. Output helps students notice the gap between what they want to say/write and what they do say/write. It helps learners notice particular forms of language, focus their attention on areas that they are struggling with, and listen more carefully to input. Output also acts as a means of testing hypotheses and trying out new language. In addition, it serves as a metalinguistic function of controlling internal knowledge to improve students' language, and helps create greater automaticity (Gass, 2003).

Figure 4.1 presents the relationship between input and output, which shows that there is an interdependence between input and output, and that the four skills are interconnected to serve the learner's interlanguage development.

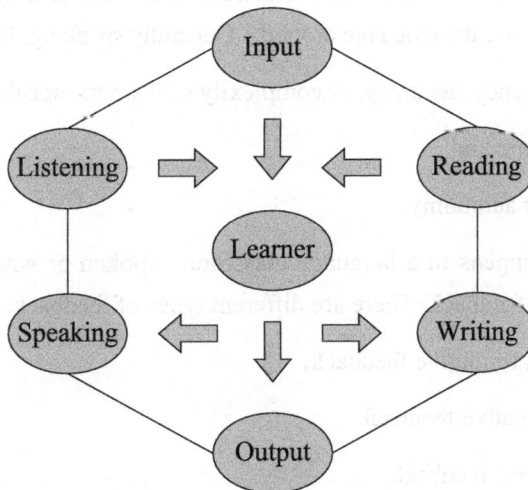

**Figure 4.1   The relationship between input and output**

Gass (2003) further explains the process of transforming input to output, which involves the following five steps:

a) First, the learner is exposed to some language.

b) Next, the learner notices some particular language features.

c) Then, the learner understands the meaning of those language features.

d) Then, the language features "go in"—they're assimilated into the learner's linguistic library of grammatical structures and vocabulary.

e) Finally, the language is available to the learner to use as output. If the learner has difficulty producing language, that then helps him/her focus and notice the next set of input. This process suggests that both input and output can help learners acquire a second language.

The Output Hypothesis says that when interacting with others, learners receive feedback from their interlocutors about what they say or write, which helps them determine what language works. Clearly, feedback is important during this process.

**Feedback** in second language acquisition is information that a learner receives about his/her language learning, and most commonly refers to information about the language he/she produces (speaking and writing), although it can also refer to reading and listening, study skills, attitudes, effort and so on. It can be used to give a general indication of proficiency in any particular skill (speaking, writing, listening or reading) or to target specific topics (grammar, vocabulary, etc.) that are new or in need of review.

Without language feedback, students cannot learn the target language because they do not know how well they are using it and whether they are using it correctly. Clearly, language feedback indicates whether students are on the correct path, whether they understand a specific point or not, and, how to use the language properly. Generally speaking, feedback serves to:

- improve the fluency, accuracy, or complexity of learners' speaking and writing;

- motivate learners; and

- develop learner autonomy.

Everything that happens in a language classroom, spoken or written, can be used and understood as language feedback. There are different types of feedback:

- summative and formative feedback,

- positive and negative feedback,

- direct and indirect feedback,

- oral and written feedback, and

- teacher, student and machine feedback.

**Summative feedback** refers to an evaluation, typically in the form of a score, of a student's work or at the end of a period of study, and **formative feedback** refers to the information that is intended to help the learner in some way and is given continuously during learning (Lee, 2017).

**Positive feedback** refers to the information about what is correct in the target language, and **negative feedback** is the information as to what is not correct in the target language.

In practice, language feedback is often concerned with correcting mistakes (i.e., corrective feedback). Hence, when considering how to provide feedback, it is important to distinguish between mistakes and errors. **Mistakes** are performance errors, where the learner knows the correct rule, word, ending, and so on, but has performed incorrectly. **Errors** occur because learners do not yet know the correct rule, word, ending, and so on, and are making guesses, often based on their native language and their current knowledge of the target language. It is important for an instructor to direct his/her language feedback toward correcting mistakes, which is what learners should be able to do in the target language. Decisions about when to provide feedback, how much and what kind of feedback to give, are based on feeling and sensing what your students need and when.

## 4.4 Knowledge types

This section mainly focuses on three types of knowledge: declarative and procedural knowledge, explicit and implicit knowledge, and knowledge representation and control.

### 4.4.1 Declarative and procedural knowledge

Declarative knowledge is knowledge about facts and things, and knowledge that something is the case. In other words, declarative knowledge can be thought of as the who, what, when, and where of information. For example, "A" is the first letter of the English alphabet, Beijing is the capital of China, and the Great Wall is one of the eight wonders of the world. Facts, world or personal history, math rules, metalinguistic knowledge, and knowledge of linguistic forms are different categories of declarative knowledge. The classroom is full of assessments of declarative knowledge like traditional tests, book reports, written or oral history reports, or language translation assignments. A key feature of declarative knowledge is that it is easy to express declarative knowledge in terms of words or symbols. Declarative knowledge is explicit, which means that the learner is consciously aware of his or her understanding of declarative information. Learners can retrieve it when called upon to do so.

Procedural knowledge involves knowing how to do something, like riding a bike, cooking a dish, and solving a problem. Procedural knowledge involves implicit learning, which a learner may not be aware of, and may involve being able to use a particular form to understand or produce language without necessarily being able to explain it. It relates to motor and cognitive skills that involve sequencing information (e.g., playing tennis, producing language) and using language (e.g., stringing words together to form and interpret sentences). A key feature of procedural knowledge is that it is difficult to explain verbally. What is very interesting is that once procedural knowledge is gained, it tends to become implicit, which means that one is no longer consciously aware of it.

Any time an assignment instruction uses verbs, the standard is addressing procedural knowledge. For example, procedural instructions ask a student to evaluate a mathematical expression, compare and contrast the plots of two literary passages, or compose an original play based on a particular period of history. "Evaluate", "compare", "contrast", and "compose" are verbs, indicating that the knowledge being assessed is procedural.

Procedural knowledge is often automated: We often begin to do something without any apparent conscious attention to what we are doing or why we are doing it. For example, as we read, we naturally decode words and comprehend the meaning of what we are reading automatically. Just as it is difficult to explain in words how to ride a bike, it is difficult to explain in actions the history of bicycling in the 20th century.

In second language teaching and learning, an important use of the declarative-procedural distinction is to describe the kinds of learning that students may achieve. For example, an EFL (English as a foreign language) learner may memorize past tense rules as declarative knowledge, but he or she may have little or no idea how these rules are actually used in speaking and writing (procedural knowledge). It is believed that, with age, the ability to use procedural knowledge to learn new operations decreases, and older second language learners need to rely more on declarative information in their learning. And of course, there is an interplay between declarative and procedural knowledge in most learning.

### 4.4.2　Explicit and implicit knowledge

Explicit knowledge is a set of rules learned by a learner just as any mechanical skill (Ellis, 1994). It is learned consciously. Explicit knowledge is accessed through controlled processing and can be accessed during planning. Explicit knowledge is the most basic form of knowledge and is easy to pass along because it's written down and accessible. When data is processed, organized, structured, and interpreted, the result is explicit knowledge. Explicit knowledge is easily articulated, recorded, communicated, and most importantly in the world of knowledge management, stored. Course papers, research reports, and data sheets are all examples of explicit knowledge.

Implicit knowledge is acquisition of knowledge about the underlying structure of a complex stimulus environment by a process which takes place naturally, simply and without conscious operations (Ellis, 1994). Practices and skills that are transferable from job to job are examples of implicit knowledge. When acquiring a grammar item implicitly, a learner does not even know that he or she is learning. Access to implicit knowledge occurs through automatic processing.

Declarative memory can be seen as the basis of explicit knowledge, and procedural knowledge underlies implicit knowledge. Implicit knowledge is the practical application of explicit knowledge. Both types of knowledge can be used by native and nonnative speakers in generating utterances, although native speakers presumably rely much less on explicit knowledge than on implicit knowledge. Through practice, exposure, drills, etc., explicit knowledge can become implicit, and vice versa.

### 4.4.3   Knowledge representation and control

Bialystok and Smith (1985) noted that there are two aspects of importance in describing knowledge of a language: knowledge representation (the level of analysis and mental organization of linguistic information) and control over that knowledge (the speed and efficiency with which that information can be accessed). They made four points about the nature of learners' grammatical knowledge and how this knowledge differs from that of native speakers in a number of ways:

a) Extent of analysis in the grammar.

b) Greater analytic sophistication does not necessarily entail greater approximation to the target language.

c) Re-analysis does not necessarily entail greater complexity (depth of analysis).

d) Greater analysis does not necessarily entail greater conscious awareness.

Increased ability to analyze target language structures does not necessarily entail correctness (Point b). In many cases, learners use prefabricated patterns or language chunks to process or produce information in the second language. Prefabricated patterns are those bits of language for which there has been no internal analysis. They enable learners to express functions which they are unable to construct from their linguistic system. As the learner's system of linguistic rules develops over time, the externally consistent prefabricated patterns are assimilated into the internal structure (Hakuta, 1976).

Re-analysis does not necessarily mean that the learner is moving in the direction of the target language, nor that the analysis has become any more complex (Point c). Point d addresses conscious awareness. The use of a system (correct or incorrect vis-à-vis TL norms) is not dependent on the learner's conscious awareness of the system or on his or her ability to articulate what the system is. What increased analysis does is to allow the learner to make greater use of the system and not necessarily increase the learner's conscious awareness of that system. Thus, determining the components of a chunked phrase allows the learner to use those component parts in other linguistic contexts. Increased awareness may or may not come as a result.

DeKeyser (1997) argues that second language learning is like other forms of learning, both cognitive and psychomotor. The basic argument is that, regardless of what one is learning (e.g., language or tennis), learning progresses from knowledge that (declarative) relating to some skill or behavior, to knowledge how (procedural), and finally to the automatization of procedural knowledge. The first type of knowledge can be obtained through observation and analysis or through verbal instruction (or both). The next step is to move from the stage of conceptualization (declarative knowledge) to using that knowledge (procedural knowledge), to some sort of performance (e.g., producing language, understanding language, swinging a tennis racket). But this is only the beginning, for procedural knowledge needs to become fast and without deliberation. Practice (whether time spent in training or time spent using an L2 in a foreign country) is necessary to ensure that particular behaviors are quick, and with diminished attention paid to the particular task (e.g., producing and/or understanding language).

## 4.5　Psycholinguistic constructs

### 4.5.1　Attention

According to the *American Heritage Dictionary*, attention refers to "the concentration of the mental powers upon an object". Attention in second language research refers to the process that encodes language input, keeps it active in working and short-term memory, and retrieves it from long-term memory. The focus of attention is a subset of short-term memory, which is part of long-term memory in a currently heightened state of activation.

Long's (1996) Interaction Hypothesis suggests that attention is one of the crucial mechanisms in the process of negotiation, which allows learners to utilize the content of the negotiation to advance their own knowledge.

Schmidt's (1990, 1994, 2001) Noticing Hypothesis also claims that attention is essential to language learning and that a learner cannot continue to develop his/her language abilities or grasp linguistic features without consciously noticing the input. Underlying this hypothesis is the idea of noticing a gap, and awareness (through attention) is necessary for this noticing. According to this hypothesis, a learner's attention is focused on a specific part of the language, specifically on those discrepancies between target language forms and learner-language forms through interaction (e.g., negotiation, recasts). Schmidt and Frota (1986: 311) suggested that "a second language learner will begin to acquire the target like form if and only if it is present in comprehended input and 'noticed' in the normal sense of the word, that is consciously".

A number of studies show a connection between awareness and learning (Leow, 1997, 2000). Yet, because the Noticing Hypothesis does not specifically target the grammar of natural language, it has been criticized for being too vague (Truscott, 1998). And Williams (2004) found that there could be learning without awareness. Thus, there is also debate over whether learners must consciously notice something, or whether the noticing can be subconscious to some degree (Lightbown & Spada, 2006).

### 4.5.2  Working memory

Working memory refers to the structures and processes that humans use to store and manipulate information. It is commonly defined as a complement to long-term memory that allows for short-term activation of information while permitting the manipulation of the information in question.

"Working memory is those mechanisms or processes that are involved in the control, regulation, and active maintenance of task-relevant information in the service of complex cognition, including novel as well as familiar, skilled tasks" (Miyake & Shah, 1999: 450).

The term that most often precedes working memory is "short-term memory". The major difference is that working memory focuses on the manipulation of information, while short-term memory focuses on the storage of information.

Baddeley and Hitch (1974) propose a model of working memory, in which there are two slave systems and a central executive responsible for system maintenance: The articulatory loop and the visuo-spatial sketch pad. The articulatory loop contains phonological information which is maintained by articulating the phonological information. For example, when you want to remember a phone number and do not have a pen and paper to write it down, you will repeat the number over and over until you can get to a phone to dial the number or find pen and paper to write it down. The visuo-spatial sketch pad stores visual and spatial information. The central executive focuses attention on some things, inhibits others, and is the overall supervisor and coordinator of information when more than one task needs to be done at a time.

Research provides convincing evidence for the importance of working memory to first and second language comprehension and acquisition. For example, Miyake and Friedman (1998) found that there was a relationship between L2 working memory and syntax comprehension. Service and Kohonen (1995) noted a relationship between phonological short-term memory capacity and the acquisition of L2 vocabulary.

### 4.5.3 Monitoring

The Monitor Hypothesis proposed by Krashen (1982) claims that a learner's acquired system of a second language is responsible for initiating speech, and the learned system acts as a monitor of what he/she is producing. The monitor allows a language user to change the form of an utterance either prior to production by consciously applying learned rules or after production via self-correction. In other words, the learned system monitors the output of the acquired system. This is shown in Figure 4.2.

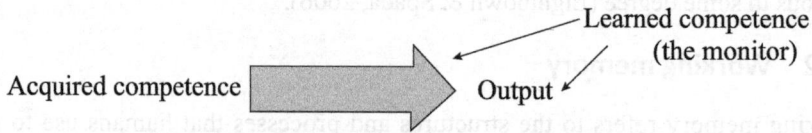

**Figure 4.2   The monitor model**

Monitoring can't be used all the time. The following are conditions for it to work effectively:

a) Time. Learners need time to consciously think about and use the rules available to them in their learned system.

b) Focus on form. Although time may be basic, the learner must also focus on form. Learners must be paying attention to how they are saying/writing something, not just to what they are saying/writing.

c) Know the rule. In order to apply a rule, the learner has to know it. In other words, the learner has to have an appropriate learned system in order to apply it.

Learners therefore monitor their spontaneous speeches/texts using their learned system. This is why self-repairs and self-corrections occur in learners' spontaneous speeches/texts. The Monitor Hypothesis also predicts faster initial progress for adults than for children, arguing that adults often enter conversations earlier than children and monitor when producing L2 utterances before having acquired the ability for natural performance. Nevertheless, in the long term, second language acquisition that starts in childhood will be superior in terms of ultimate attainment.

# Tasks

## 1. Explain the following terms.

interlanguage                          fossilization                  language transfer

positive transfer                      negative transfer              Contrastive Analysis Hypothesis

Markedness Differential Hypothesis     input                          interaction

output                                 positive evidence              negative evidence

foreigner talk                         interlanguage talk             feedback

mistake                                declarative knowledge          procedural knowledge

explicit knowledge                     implicit knowledge             attention

Noticing Hypothesis                    working memory                 monitor

## 2. Read the following statements and decide whether they are true (√) or false (x).

1) Every learner's interlanguage is largely similar. (   )

2) Fossilization occurs for definite reasons. (   )

3) Language transfer seldom occurs from L2 to L1 or from L3 to L2. (   )

4) Normally, whatever happens in a classroom that is directed towards learners is feedback. (   )

5) When teachers have students identify the main characters, plot, and setting of a story, they are assessing declarative knowledge. (   )

6) Writing out definitions to vocabulary words or formulas in math are examples of assessing procedural knowledge. (   )

7) Declarative knowledge hardly becomes procedural knowledge. (   )

8) Learning never happens without attention. (   )

## 3. Discuss the following questions.

1) Why does fossilization occur? Can fossilization disappear?

2) What are examples of positive language transfer?

3) What are the roles of input? What does input imply for classroom teaching and learning?

4) What are the roles of interaction?

5) What are the roles of output? What does output imply for classroom teaching and learning?

6) What are the roles of feedback? What does feedback imply for classroom teaching and learning?

7) How can declarative knowledge become procedural knowledge?

8) Do you agree that a learner's tendency to monitor his/her own form gets in the way of acquiring the language?

## 4. Projects.

1) What do you think of the role of monitor in second language learning? Illustrate your ideas with data from second language learners.

2) Is there any transfer from Chinese to your learning of English as a FL? Is the transfer negative or positive? Examine the types and effects of language transfer with data from second language learners.

3) How do students feel about feedback in second language writing? What types of feedback do students prefer on their second language writing? Please design a study to find out how students perceive feedback and how effective the feedback is to their second language writing.

language

culture

learning

hello

world

UNIT

**5**

# Instructed second language learning

## Objectives

In this unit, you will learn

—different aspects of classroom environment (e.g., features of classroom language, traditional instruction and processing instruction, and the Teachability/Learnability Hypothesis);

—focus on form/forms/meaning;

—effectiveness of instruction.

## 5.1　Classroom environment

Formal second language teaching and learning usually takes place in classrooms. Then, what is the difference between classroom teaching and learning and that in the natural environment/naturalistic learning? Basically, they are different in at least four aspects:

- the teacher,
- the learners,
- the classroom environment, and
- input.

For example, in most second language classrooms, input mainly comes from three sources: a) the teacher, b) the materials, and c) other learners. Input can be found everywhere in the naturalistic learning of the native language.

### 5.1.1　Classroom language

Since teachers have to interact with learners at various points in the classroom in order to engage them psychologically and emotionally in the learning process, teachers' language, also called teacher talk, is an important source of input in second language classrooms.

The general features of teacher talk include (Anandan, 2014: 22):

- using error-free language with well-formed constructions;
- using language that is comprehensible to all learners;
- being audible to the whole class;
- using language that is dynamic, positive, pleasant and learner-friendly;
- using language that is free of expressions related to finding fault with the learners;

- drastically reducing the speed of articulation;

- maintaining articulatory features (such as pause, stress, tone, and tempo);

- making sure that there is a dialogue between the teacher and the learners and not just one-sided talk from the teacher;

- using language that contains various discourse markers (such as "such", "as well", "precisely", "as a matter of fact", etc.) wherever these elements are required contextually;

- using language that contains linguistic elements (such as tags, short responses, etc.);

- addressing higher order thinking skills.

Meanwhile, teachers' language varies as students' proficiency in the second language increases, as shown in Table 5.1.

**Table 5.1    Complexity of teacher speech directed at different proficiency levels (Gaies, 1979: 190)**

| Level | Words per T-unit | Ratio of clauses to T-units[*] | Words per clause |
|---|---|---|---|
| Beginner | 4.30 | 1.02 | 4.20 |
| Upper beginner | 5.75 | 1.14 | 5.04 |
| Intermediate | 6.45 | 1.24 | 5.18 |
| Advanced | 8.26 | 1.38 | 5.98 |
| Baseline | 10.97 | 1.60 | 6.84 |

*T-units are defined as "one main clause plus any subordinate clause or non-clausal structure that is attached to or embedded in it" (Hunt, 1970: 4).

Likewise, learners' language is also an important source of input in second language classrooms. In many cases, learners' language can be good input for other learners. For example, Bruton and Samuda (1980) listened to 10 hours of taped conversations, and found only one example of a change from a correct to an incorrect form. They claimed that errors from classmates might not be incorporated into a learner's grammar. This may be because learners know when they are right and may also know when they are wrong, or at least have a sense that they are not sure. Nevertheless, as discussed in Unit 3, learners' language cannot always serve as good input for other learners due to the characteristics of interlanguage.

### 5.1.2    Traditional instruction and processing instruction

In formal second language classrooms, instruction plays a crucial role. Traditional instruction is the instructional method widely used in most foreign language classrooms, which consists of a progression from mechanical drills, to meaningful drills, and finally to communicative drills (Fernández, 2011). It emphasizes teaching grammatical rules explicitly to learners, and focuses on the manipulation of learner output (VanPatten & Cadierno, 1993). That is, instruction occurs by explaining a grammatical concept and then having learners practice producing a given structure or form, as shown in Figure 5.1.

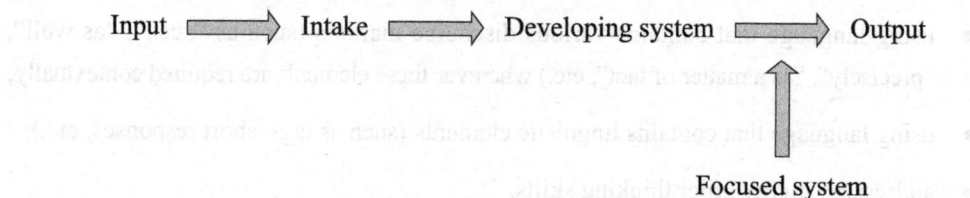

Input $\Longrightarrow$ Intake $\Longrightarrow$ Developing system $\Longrightarrow$ Output

Focused system

**Figure 5.1    Traditional instruction in foreign language learning**
(VanPatten & Cadierno, 1993)

Traditional instruction has been criticized for two main reasons: a) It forces learners to produce grammatical forms before they are linguistically capable of doing so, and b) it includes mechanical drills which are devoid of meaning and do not facilitate learners' making of necessary form-meaning connections required for acquisition to take place (Wong & VanPatten, 2003). Even so, output-based instruction continues to be the dominant form of instruction in foreign language classrooms (Fernández, 2011).

Processing instruction (PI) refers to a particular type of input-based grammar instruction, specifically designed to help learners link and acquire grammatical forms and meanings in a second language effectively through the provision of input (VanPatten, 1996, 2004). It moves learners away from incorrect processing strategies and towards optimal processing of input.

PI involves giving learners explicit information of target grammatical forms briefly and then guiding them to mentally process the meaning manifested in the use of certain grammatical forms (Wong, 2004). Namely, it deals with the conversion of input into intake and specifically focuses on form-meaning relations (VanPatten, 1995; VanPatten & Cadierno, 1993), as shown in Figure 5.2.

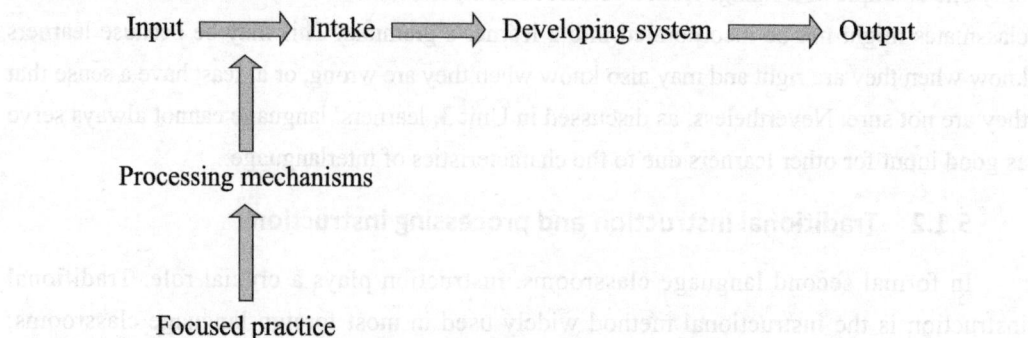

Input $\Longrightarrow$ Intake $\Longrightarrow$ Developing system $\Longrightarrow$ Output

Processing mechanisms

Focused practice

**Figure 5.2    Processing instruction in foreign language teaching**
(VanPatten & Cadierno, 1993)

According to VanPattern (2000), PI has three basic features:

a) Giving learners information about a structure or form;

b) Informing learners about a particular processing strategy that may get in the way of selecting the form/structure during comprehension; and

c) Structuring input so that learners must rely on form/structure to get meaning and not rely on natural processing tendencies.

A key feature of PI is structured input, which is manipulated in order to pinpoint the communicative value of grammatical forms. Structured input can be created by removing lexical redundancies. For example, in Example 5.1, ESL (English as second language) learners may not need to notice or process the bound inflectional morpheme "-ed" because the lexical item "yesterday" conveys a past tense meaning.

### Example 5.1

Teddy walked for two hours in the park yesterday.

In order to pinpoint the communicative value of the targeted grammatical form, i.e., past tense, the redundant lexical item "yesterday" should be removed. Without this word, learners would be forced to notice and process the grammatical morpheme "-ed" to extract meaning (temporal reference) of past tense.

Input processing occurs when learners make a form-meaning connection, which connects a grammatical form and the referential meaning that it encodes (e.g., -ed = past tense). Research has shown that PI is (highly) effective, especially in learning difficult aspects of grammar in the second language (Benati & Lee, 2008; Lee & Benati, 2007; VanPatten, 1993, 1996, 2004).

VanPatten (2008) presents three premises that form the basis of processing instruction:

a) Learners need input for acquisition;

b) A major problem in acquisition might be the way in which learners process input;

c) If we can understand how learners process input, then we might be able to devise effective input enhancement or focus on form to aid the acquisition of formal features of language.

A comparison of traditional instruction and processing instruction indicates that (Benati, 2016):

- processing instruction seems to directly affect learners' ability to process input and thus is a more effective pedagogical intervention than traditional instruction;

- processing instruction helps increase learners' rate of processing, i.e., L2 learners are able to interpret sentences efficiently and correctly;

- processing instruction helps increase the rate of accuracy in production, i.e., L2 learners are able to produce the target linguistic features during output practice.

### 5.1.3 The Teachability/Learnability Hypothesis

Krashen's Natural Order Hypothesis claims that the elements of language (or language rules) are acquired in a predictable order. The order is the same regardless of whether or not instruction is involved. This implies that pedagogical intervention cannot change (or can change in only a trivial manner) natural acquisition orders. Namely, instructions need to be geared to learners' natural developmental stages to be more effective. Based on this idea, Pieneman (1989) proposes the **Teachability Hypothesis**.

The Teachability Hypothesis suggests that the natural developmental sequence (e.g., *wh-*questions, some grammatical morphemes, negation, possessive determiners, relative clause, etc.) cannot be altered by instruction for elements of language whose acquisition is governed by universal processing constraints, but other variational features of language, i.e., those that have no developmental level of acquisition and can be acquired at any point in time, can be successfully taught at any stage of development. Thus, teachers need to be familiar with the order and sequence of acquisition that learners in general manifest and the developmental stage that individual learners have reached. Pienemann (1989) argues that the teachability of language is constrained by what the learner is ready to acquire, because "some structures are best learned if the specific instruction coincides with the learners' next stage of development" (Ollerhead & Oosthuizen, 2005: 62). Namely, two basic ideas of the Teachability Hypothesis are:

- developmental sequences are determined and controlled by constraints on processing;

- formal instruction is effective in helping learners acquire specific forms to the extent that learners are ready for it.

Pienemann (1989) also proposes the **Learnability Hypothesis**, which states that the classroom instruction is beneficial to learners only to the degree that they are psycholinguistically ready for it. The Learnability Hypothesis exerts some constraints on the Teachability Hypothesis, which means that the effectiveness of teaching is limited to the learning for which the learner is ready. On the other hand, what is learnable can be teachable. It calls for an awareness of the sequence and order of learners' acquisition and their developmental stage to determine their readiness in acquiring certain language features on the part of language teachers.

The Teachability/Learnability Hypothesis receives much support (see Table 5.2), yet it also faces criticisms due to two reasons: a) It is difficult to determine learners' "current state of grammar" or interlanguage, and b) Learners' interlanguage develops in a sequence different from that introduced by the teacher (Kumaravadivelu, 2006).

**Table 5.2    Support for the Teachability Hypothesis**

| Study | Descriptions | Results |
|---|---|---|
| Krashen (1982) | Input should be slightly above the learner's current level: "i+1". | |
| Pienemann (1987) | Investigated whether instruction permitted learners to skip a stage in the natural order of development through instruction. | Learners could not skip steps and learn developmental features until they were ready. |
| Mackay & Philip (1998) | Studied whether adult learners at different developmental stages could progress their formation of questions if instruction used recast as a method of corrective feedback. | Only learners who were ready and received recasts excelled in the production of question forms. |
| Spada & Lightbown (1999) | Explored the acquisition of questions based on learner readiness. | Length of instruction affected learners' developmental readiness; first language might interfere with learners' readiness. |
| McDonough (2005) | Investigated the impact of negative feedback in Thai ESL learners by examining question development. | Learners would increase the stage over a long period of time. |
| Kim (2012) | Examined if increasing the level of complexity in a task would promote greater interaction by comparing Korean university students in an English and a second-language class. If this was true, would it contribute to L2 development? | The higher the task was in terms of complexity, the greater number of language-related episodes which strengthened question structures and language development. |

## 5.2  Focus on form/forms/meaning

Focus on form, focus on forms and focus on meaning are three different approaches to language education.

### 5.2.1  Focus on form

Focus on form, proposed by Long (1988), refers to a need for meaning-focused activity in which attention to form is embedded. It consists of primarily meaning-focused interaction in which there is brief and sometimes spontaneous attention to linguistic forms (Loewen,

2018). Focus on form assumes that acquisition occurs best when learners' attention is drawn to language items when they are needed for communication. It is a central construct in task-based language teaching (Ellis, 2016). Types of focus on form include input flood, input enhancement, and corrective feedback. According to Shintani (2013), focus on form has the following features:

- The primary focus is on meaning (i.e., message processing) rather than on form.

- It involves an occasional shift of the learners' attention from meaning to linguistic form.

- It emphasizes form-function mapping.

- It can involve a variety of instructional activities.

### 5.2.2 Focus on forms

Focus on forms refers to earlier teaching methodologies in which the main organizing principle for language instruction was the accumulation of individual language items (e.g., plural endings, passives) (Long, 1991). It emphasizes the role of explicit knowledge of language features in the acquisition process. It involves a primary emphasis on linguistic structures, often presented as discrete grammar rules or other metalinguistic information (Loewen, 2018). Types of focus on forms include present, practice, produce (PPP), and explicit language instruction. It lacks support from empirical research in that learners typically acquire language features in sequences and their interlanguage at different stages often exhibits non-native-like language forms. According to researchers (Long, 1991; Ur, 1996), focus on forms has the following features:

- Language is broken down into discrete elements (e.g., words, grammar rules, notions, functions), which are then taught item by item in a linear, additive fashion.

- It involves a linear syllabus, instructional materials, and corresponding procedures designed to present and practice a series of linguistic items.

- Learners' primary attention is directed at linguistic form, but meaning is not excluded.

- It is realized in the form of present-practice-produce (PPP).

- PPP seeks to elicit the production of correct target forms right from the outset as a means for learning them.

For an instructional intervention to qualify as *focus on form* rather than a *focus on forms*, the learner must be aware of the meaning and use of the language features before the form is brought to their attention. In second language classrooms, there are numerous such examples, as shown in Example 5.2.

*Example 5.2*

> Student (S): She finally success.
>
> Teacher (T): What?
>
> S: She finally succeed.
>
> T: Succeeds.
>
> S: Yes.

Although the student does not appreciate the full force of the teacher's indirect question, he/she understands that the teacher is making a correction of form, and thus modifies his/her original utterance accordingly. Yet, it is unclear whether the "yes" indicates anything more than the closure to the exchange.

Williams (1999) investigated eight classroom learners at different levels of proficiency. The study identified numerous examples of learner-generated attention to form and considerable variation. The results showed that learners at low levels of proficiency did not often spontaneously attend to language form. Williams and Evans (1998) investigated the effect of focus on form on two structures: (a) participial adjectives of emotive verbs ("I am boring" vs. "I am bored"), and (b) passives ("The dog was chased by the cat"). Three groups of learners took part in this study: One group received explicit instruction and feedback, the second group received input only, and the third group served as the control. The overall results suggested that learners' "readiness" contributed to their ability to focus on and take in new information, and that not all structures were created equal with regard to input type.

It is clear that learner-generated attention to form may not always come naturally and, clearly, may require some pedagogical training. Not all grammatical constructions can be taught with a focus-on-form instruction. For example, some structures are so complex, involving movement, that it is not at all clear as to what could be focused on.

Then, it can be concluded that:

- instructed learning can provide a context for focus on form. This does not mean that all forms are "teachable";
- different kinds of input might be necessary.

Doughty and Williams (1998) outlined four areas to consider in the study of focus on form: timing, forms to focus on, input manipulation, and input enhancement. Based on a review of several studies on timing issues, Lightbown (1998) cautioned researchers/teachers not to take the notion of developmental sequences too seriously within a pedagogical context. Namely, while it may be the case that input on stages that may be considerably beyond the learner's current level does not lead to learning, there is no harm done to the learner. What is relevant, however, is the need for teachers to have appropriate expectations of what learners will and will not be able to take away from a lesson that includes input on stages well beyond their levels.

### 5.2.3    Focus on meaning

Focus on meaning is "an approach to language teaching that emphasizes implicit language learning where learners' focus of attention is on meaning" (Long, 1991). In a focus-on-meaning approach, "learners are usually not specifically taught the strategies, maxims and organizational principles that govern communicative language use but are expected to work these out for themselves through extensive task engagement" (Celce-Murcia et al., 1997: 141). According to Krashen (1981), focus on meaning is the key factor in successful second language acquisition. In a focus-on-meaning approach, learners learn a second language best when they experience it as a means of communication, and incidental and implicit learning is sufficient for language acquisition. Therefore, explicit attention to linguistic items and awareness are not required for successful language acquisition. Hence, this approach emphasizes providing opportunities for learners to experience rich input (Norris & Ortega, 2000).

### 5.2.4    Input enhancement

Focus on form "overtly draws students' attention to linguistic elements as they arise incidentally in lessons whose overriding focus is on meaning or communication" (Long, 1991: 45–46). This is similar to enhanced input proposed by Sharwood Smith (1993), which refers to the input that is enhanced by an external source (e.g., a teacher) or an internal source (learners drawing on their own resources). Input enhancement is a pedagogical intervention that aims to help L2 learners notice specific forms in the input (Smith, 1993). Leow (2001) defines enhanced input as input that has been altered typologically to enhance the saliency of target forms.

Input enhancement aims to encourage learners to detect particular linguistic features, consciously or unconsciously, so that their focus on meaning is not disrupted. To realize input enhancement, salient features of particular linguistic features should be emphasized to learners, like color-coding affixes or providing aural as well as visual input (Long, 2017). Input enhancement varies in terms of explicitness and elaboration. One technique is modifying a text so that a particular target item would appear over and over again. In this way, the text will contain many exemplars of the same feature (input flood). Another technique is underlying, italicizing, or capitalizing a specific grammatical item (providing typographical cues) in a text (textual enhancement). Input enhancement techniques expose learners to comprehensible input and positive evidence while at the same time directing their attention to specific linguistic properties of the target language (Wong, 2005).

As discussed in Han (2005), input enhancement has the following roles:

- Simple enhancement is capable of inducing the learner to notice externally enhanced forms in meaning-bearing input. Whether or not this leads to acquisition depends largely on the learner's readiness.

- Learners can automatically notice forms that are meaningful.

- Simple enhancement of a longer term is more likely to incite learners to notice the target form than simple enhancement of a shorter term.

- Simple enhancement is more likely to induce learners to notice the target form when it is sequential to comprehension than when it is concurrent with comprehension.

- Simple enhancement of a non-meaningful form does not interfere with comprehension.

- Simple enhancement of a meaningful form contributes to comprehension.

- Simple enhancement is more effective if it draws focal rather than peripheral attention.

- Simple enhancement, when combined with input flood, is likely to evoke aberrant noticing, resulting in overuse of the enhanced form.

- Compound enhancement (combining different types of enhancement, e.g., typographical enhancement with feedback) is more likely to induce deeper cognitive processing than simple enhancement, possibly to the extent of engendering "overlearning".

Input flood has the following effects (Benati, 2016: 70):

- Input flood might be effective in increasing learners' knowledge of what is possible in the target language.

- Input flood might be an effective instructional technique subject to factors such as the length of treatment and the nature of linguistic feature.

- Input flood might not be effective in increasing learners' knowledge of what is not possible in the target language.

VanPatten (1996) stated that while input flood could increase the chances that an L2 learner would notice a specific target form, it did not guarantee noticing.

A significant function of language instruction is the manipulation of input. That is, teachers can vary the degree of explicitness in the input.

## 5.3 Effectiveness of instruction

Understanding the effectiveness of instruction entails an analysis of the type of instruction. For example, is it explicit or implicit? Does it focus on meaning, form, or forms?

Based on a review of instructed second language acquisition, Norris and Ortega (2000) concluded that explicit focus was more effective than implicit focus and that a focus on form was more effective than a focus on forms. Nevertheless, it is worth noting that these findings should be treated with caution because of the following reasons: (a) The measurements of learning outcomes in the studies they included tended to favor explicit treatments; (b) Implicit treatments might require a longer period of time for learning to take place and consequently might necessitate longer post-observation periods than explicit treatments; and (c) there was often an inconsistent operationalization of each instructional approach. Finally, the linguistic forms targeted in most of the studies reviewed were (relatively) easy and simple, which potentially favored explicit explanation. Yet, Truscott (2004) reached different conclusions about the effectiveness of instruction based on his analysis of Norris and Ortega (2000).

Ellis and Wulff (2015) claim that the role of instruction is limited. It can facilitate the development of "noticing" target forms, which might not be salient in the input language learners are exposed to. Yet, it is not always effective due to different factors (e.g., learners are not psycholinguistically ready, there is a mismatch between explicit knowledge and implicit mental representation, learner aptitude, etc.).

Based on a review of contemporary views on the role of instruction in second language acquisition, Benati (2016) got the following conclusions:

- Instruction does not alter the route of acquisition (i.e., acquisition orders and developmental sequences).

- Instruction might speed up the rate of acquisition.

The effectiveness of instruction is not a matter of yes or no, but a clearer understanding of what, how, and when (in terms of a learner's developmental readiness). These are all areas that must be addressed empirically. Beyond the mere focus on form, forms or meaning, explicitness or implicitness of input, numerous other variables affect the effectiveness of instruction, like the learning environment and individual differences. There are no simple answers. What is clear is that instruction does make a difference, but how precisely it makes a difference and what factors contribute to its effectiveness are still questions that need to be researched.

# Tasks

## 1. Explain the following terms.

Teachability Hypothesis          Learnability Hypothesis          processing instruction

traditional instruction          focus on forms                   focus on meaning

focus on form                    input enhancement

## 2. Read the following statements and decide whether they are true (√) or false (×).

1) The input in second language classrooms is similar to that in the natural environment learning. (   )

2) Learner talk serves as good input for other learners. (   )

3) Teacher talk varies as students' proficiency in the second language changes. (   )

4) Traditional instruction focuses on manipulation of input. (   )

5) Traditional instruction forces learners to produce grammatical forms before they are linguistically ready. (   )

6) Processing instruction helps learners learn target grammatical forms by giving learners implicit information. (   )

7) Teachers always know at what stages their students are and whether they are ready to learn new forms. (   )

8) Instruction does no harm to learners even if they are not psycho-linguistically ready to learn new forms. (   )

## 3. Discuss the following questions.

1) What are the features of teacher talk?

2) How is processing instruction different from traditional instruction?

3) What are the features of processing instruction?

4) What are the features of focus on form?

5) What are the features of focus on forms?

6) What do you think of the relationship between second language acquisition and second language pedagogy? How are they different? How might they affect each other? Relate your answers to a specific learning situation.

7) Are all structures equally amenable to focus on form? Why or why not? Can you give examples from your own learning experience when you could not figure out what the correct generalization should be?

8) What do you think of the effectiveness of instruction? Relate your answer to a specific learning situation.

## 4. Projects.

1) What do you think of the Teachability Hypothesis? Please design a small study to prove/disapprove the hypothesis.

2) Which one is more effective, focus on form or focus on forms? Collect data from your peers in a specific learning situation to support your argument.

3) Is input enhancement practiced in textbooks? Select a textbook to analyze how input is enhanced and how this enhancement affects students' learning.

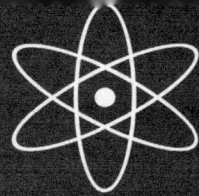

language

culture

learning

hello

world

UNIT

6

Individual differences
and second language
acquisition

# Objectives

In this unit, you will learn

—what is intelligence and how it is related to second/foreign language learning;

—what is language aptitude and how it is related to second/foreign language learning;

—what is attitude and how it is related to second/foreign language learning;

—what is motivation and how it is related to second/foreign language learning;

—what is anxiety and how it is related to second/foreign language learning;

—what is strategy and how it is related to second/foreign language learning.

In second language acquisition, it is often the case that some learners almost achieve the native level of competence while others never seem to progress much beyond a beginner's level. Some learners make rapid and apparently effortless progress while others progress (very) slowly and with (great) difficulty. All these lie in the fact that the level of second language acquisition depends on various internal and external factors. Internal factors mainly refer to individual characteristics, which play an important role in SL/FL learning (Skehan, 1989). They are age, gender, intelligence, language aptitude, motivation, anxiety, attitude, personality, strategy, learning style, and so on. Since each individual is different, they vary in these internal factors. Due to individual differences, their language learning outcomes differ even though they learn the language in the same or similar environment. Hence, individual differences have always been a focus of teaching and research in the field of second language acquisition. The differences to be briefly explored in this unit are: intelligence, language aptitude, attitude, L2 motivation, foreign language anxiety, and language learning strategies.

## 6.1 Intelligence

Since the early 1900s, psychologists have become interested in intelligence (Spearman, 1904). Spearman (1904) noticed that people who did well in one area of intelligence tests (e.g., mathematics) also did well in other areas. He thus proposed the term "general intelligence", also known as the "g-factor", which refers to a general mental ability that underlies multiple specific skills, including verbal, spatial, numerical, and mechanical skills. According to Spearman (cited in Thomson, 1947), there is a single "g-factor" which represents an individual's general intelligence across multiple abilities, and a second factor, "s", which refers to an individual's specific ability in one particular area.

Since then, the concept of intelligence has undergone lots of variation and expansion. Thurstone (1938, cited in Sternberg, 2003) challenged the concept of a g-factor and identified seven primary mental abilities that comprise intelligence: verbal comprehension, verbal fluency, number facility, spatial visualization, perceptual speed, memory, and inductive reasoning.

Gardner (1983, 1987) proposed eight multiple intelligences: linguistic, logical-mathematical, spatial, musical, bodily-kinesthetic, interpersonal, intrapersonal, and naturalistic. Gardner claims that most activities (e.g., swimming) involve a combination of these multiple intelligences (e.g., spatial and bodily-kinesthetic intelligence). He indicates that these multiple intelligences can help us understand concepts beyond intelligence, such as creativity and leadership.

Psychologist Robert Sternberg defined intelligence as "the mental abilities necessary for adaptation to, as well as shaping and selection of, any environmental context" (1997: 1). He proposed that intelligence has three aspects: analytical, creative, and practical (Sternberg, 1985). **Analytical intelligence** refers to intelligence used to analyze or evaluate problems and arrive at solutions; **creative intelligence** is the ability to go beyond what is given to create novel and interesting ideas, which involves imagination, innovation and problem-solving; **practical intelligence** is the ability to solve problems faced in daily life (Ruhl, 2020).

Along with the proposal of the concept, a number of measures have been developed to assess intelligence, some of which are described below.

**A. Binet-Simon Scale**

Psychologist Alfred Binet and his colleague Theodore Simon developed the **Binet-Simon Scale**, which became the basis for intelligence tests still in use today (Binet et al., 1912). The Binet-Simon Scale (BSS) comprised 30 items designed to measure judgment, comprehension, and reasoning, which Binet deemed the key characteristics of intelligence (Ruhl, 2020).

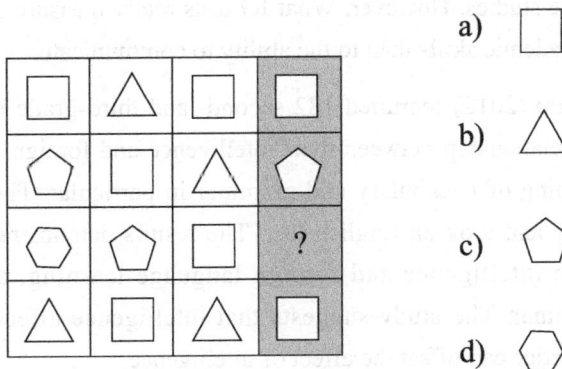

**Figure 6.1    A sample BSS IQ item**

### B. Stanford-Binet Intelligence Scale

Stanford psychologist Lewis Terman adapted the BSS for American students and published the **Stanford-Binet Intelligence Scale** (SBIS) in 1916 (Cherry, 2020). The SBIS measures intelligence according to five features of cognitive ability, including fluid reasoning, knowledge, quantitative reasoning, visual-spatial processing, and working memory. Both verbal and nonverbal responses are measured (Ruhl, 2020). The average score for the test is 100, and any score from 90 to 109 is in the Average intelligence range; a score from 110 to 119 is in the High Average range, superior scores range from 120 to 129 and a score over 130 is considered Very Superior.

### C. The Wechsler Intelligence Scale for Children

The Wechsler Intelligence Scale for Children (WISC), developed by David Wechsler, is an IQ test designed to measure intelligence and cognitive ability in children between the ages of 6 and 16, including verbal comprehension, perceptual reasoning, working memory, and processing speed (Cherry, 2020).

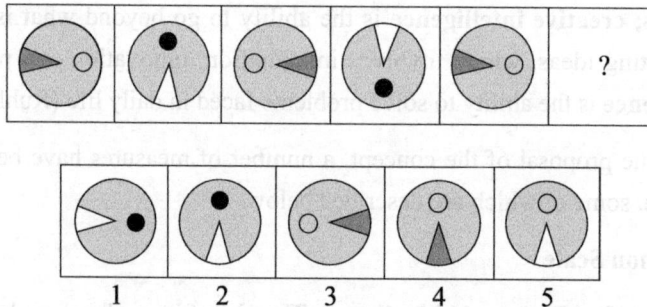

**Figure 6.2 WISC-IV sample test question**

There is a folk perception that IQ is positively related to language learning ability, and indeed the correlation coefficient between language aptitude test scores and IQ test scores is 60 or above in some studies. However, What IQ tests really measure may be more closely related to cognitive/academic skills than to the ability to communicate.

Salehi and Sadighi (2012) recruited 182 second- and third-grade high school students and investigated the relationship between their intelligence and foreign language learning in general, and the learning of vocabulary and grammar in particular. The students answered an intelligence survey and took an English test. The results demonstrated a weak positive relationship between intelligence and foreign language learning, and the learning of vocabulary and grammar. The study suggests that intelligence affects foreign language learning, but extra practice can offset the effect of intelligence.

Ghonchepour and Moghaddam (2018) investigated the relationship between intelligence and learning English in general, and learning grammar and reading comprehension in particular. Participants were 60 teenage Iranian learners, aged 15 to 19, from Kerman high schools in the second grade who took standardized tests. The study revealed a positive correlation between verbal and nonverbal intelligence and learners' English language development. Another finding was that the relationship between intelligence scores and comprehension and grammar scores was significant across all groups. The researchers claim that intelligence is one of the important factors in the acquisition of English as a foreign language, but not the only factor.

## 6.2  Language aptitude

Aptitude is "what allows people to learn easily and quickly" (Brown & Attardo, 2008: 228). According to Cronbach and Snow (1977), aptitude is sensitive to environmental factors and is either activated or inhibited as a function of the properties of different learning conditions. Hence, "no instruction/treatment is effective for all learners, and maximal effects are achievable only when there is a fit between a learner's cognitive profile and the characteristics of the instructional context." (Li, 2015: 366).

Language aptitude refers to a set of cognitive abilities that are "predictive of how well, relative to other individuals, an individual can learn a foreign language in a given amount of time and under given conditions" (Carroll & Sapon, 2002: 23). According to Carroll (1981), language aptitude has four factors or aspects: phonemic coding ability (i.e., the ability to associate sound and symbols, or the ability to spell well in alphabetic languages), grammatical sensitivity (e.g., being good at grammar), inductive language learning ability (i.e., the ability to notice patterns and relationships and to extrapolate from examples), and rote-learning ability (e.g., the ability to learn lists easily and quickly). Carroll (1981) states that language aptitude is relatively stable and hard to modify and that people differ widely in their capacity to learn foreign languages easily and rapidly.

Generally, language aptitude is measured by the Modern Language Aptitude Test (MLAT), developed by Harvard psychologist John Carroll and linguist Stanley Sapon in the 1950s and now owned by the non-profit entity Language Learning and Testing Foundation. The test can be used to predict success in learning all basic communication skills, but particularly speaking and listening. Example 6.1 is a sample MLAT question.

### Example 6.1

Now I will teach you some numbers in the new language. First, we will learn some single-digit numbers:

"ba" is "one"

"baba" is "two"

"dee" is "three"

Now I will say the name of the number in the new language, and you write down the number you hear. Try to do so before I tell you the answer:

"ba"—that was "one"

"dee"—that was "three"

"baba"—that was "two"

Now we will learn some two-digit numbers:

"tu" is "twenty"

"ti" is "thirty"

"tu-ba" is "twenty-one" in this language—because "tu" is twenty and "ba" is one. "ti-ba" is "thirty-one"—because "ti" is thirty and "ba" is one.

Now let's begin. Write down the number you hear. (You have only about 5 seconds to write down your answer)

a. ti-ba

b. ti-dee

c. baba

d. tu-dee

Researchers have shown that language aptitude is related to foreign language learning achievements (Brown & Attardo, 2008; Li, 2015). Li (2015) did a meta-analysis of 33 study reports on the role of language aptitude in second language grammar acquisition, which generated 309 effect sizes and involved 3,106 L2 learners. The analyses revealed that language aptitude showed an overall moderate association with L2 grammar learning ($r = .31$). Further analyses demonstrated that high school students were more likely to draw on language aptitude than university students and that language aptitude was more strongly correlated with explicit treatments than implicit treatments.

## 6.3 Attitude

Attitude is usually defined as a disposition or tendency to respond positively or negatively toward a certain thing such as an idea, object, person, or situation (Hosseini & Pourmandnia, 2013). Students often have positive or negative attitudes toward the language they want to learn or the people who speak it. Having positive attitudes toward tests is also claimed to be one of the reasons that make students perform better on the tests (Malallah, 2000). Parents' attitudes affect their children's attitudes in school; peers influence each other in their choice of the variety of the target language; teachers' attitudes affect students' attitudes toward language learning as well (Brown & Attardo, 2008).

The attitudes toward English Scale developed by Gardner (1985) investigate students' attitudes toward the target language. It is proposed that a more positive attitude toward the target language may lead to more authentic communication in that language and greater motivation to study the language (Gardner, 1985).

Malallah (2000) examined attitudes toward English of 409 students enrolled at Kuwait University. The study showed that students from the College of Science had the most favorable attitudes toward learning English and the most positive attitudes toward English and native speakers of English. Students from the College of Arts had less preference for learning English, but made the most effort in learning English. They had positive attitudes toward English and toward native speakers of English.

## 6.4 Language learning motivation

Initiated by Gardner and Lambert, motivation has become a distinguished research topic in second language acquisition (Dörnyei, 1990; Spolsky, 2000). Language learning motivation is "the extent to which the individual works or strives to learn the language because of a desire to do so and the satisfaction experienced in this activity" (Gardner, 1985). This definition subsumes three components of language learning motivation: The willingness to learn a second language, the effort expended and the satisfaction one can get from the learning process. Gardner (1985; Gardner & Lambert, 1972) distinguishes integrative motivation from instrumental motivation and believes that both play an important role in language learning while integrative motivation plays a greater role. Integrative motivation refers to the "motivation to learn a second language because of positive feelings toward the community that speaks that language" (Gardner, 1985: 82–83), reflecting the "individual's willingness and interest in social interaction with members of other groups" (Gardner & MacIntyre, 1993: 159). Instrumental motivation "is more self-oriented in the sense that a person prepares to learn a new code in order to derive benefits of a non-interpersonal sort (Gardner, 1985: 83)". It is more concerned with functional reasons for learning a language, like getting a better job or a promotion.

To measure language learning motivation, Gardner (1985) developed the 121-item five-point Likert Attitude/Motivation Test Battery (AMTB). The AMTB has been extensively used in various empirical research, which consistently confirms that motivation is significantly positively related to L2 learning outcomes (Belmechri & Hummel, 1998; Dörnyei, 1990, 2005; Spolsky, 2000).

As more research has been done on foreign language learning motivation, different theories like the Self-Determination Theory (Deci & Ryan, 1985) and the L2 Motivational System (Dörnyei, 2005, 2009), and concepts like extrinsic and intrinsic motivation and amotivation (Deci & Ryan, 1985) have emerged during the process. Nevertheless, integrative and instrumental motivation continue to be two fundamental concepts of language learning motivation, despite that learners confide to study a L2 for various reasons.

In addition to the AMTB and other questionnaires, interviews and diaries are often used to explore language learning motivation at a particular time point or across time (Hernández, 2010; Humphreys & Spratt, 2008; Liu, 2016). Table 6.1 presents some studies on language learning motivation, which shows that: a) Motivation is a critical factor in L2 learning; b) Learners study a L2 for diverse motivations; c) Motivation interacts with other factors; and d) Motivation is dynamic.

**Table 6.1    Example studies on language learning motivation**

| Study | Participants | Instruments | Main findings |
|---|---|---|---|
| Gardner, Lalonde & Moorcroft (1985) | 170 college learners of French in Canada | ATMB tests | (1) Students with high integrative motivation learned faster; (2) Students with more positive affective predispositions worked harder and were more interested in learning. |
| Strong (1984) | 86 kindergarten kids learning English | Interview | Children already relatively fluent in English did show a significantly greater desire to interact with Anglos. |
| Dörnyei (1990) | 134 Hungarian EFL learners | Adapted ATMB | Instrumental motives significantly contribute to motivation in FLL contexts. |
| Clément, Dörnyei, & Noels (1994) | 301 Grade 11 Hungarian EFL learners | ATMB, teacher rating | Achievement in English was significantly related to self-confidence, evaluation of the learning environment, and motivational indices. |
| Gao et al. (2004) | 2,278 Chinese college EFL learners | Self-developed questionnaires | (1) Students studied English for various motivations; (2) Students with higher motivations of intrinsic interest, going abroad, individual development and information media made more efforts in their English learning; (3) Motivation interacted with other variables such as identity change. |

(Continued)

| Study | Participants | Instruments | Main findings |
|---|---|---|---|
| Liu (2007) | 202 Chinese 3rd-year college EFL learners | Self-developed questionnaire based on ATMB | (1) Students had positive attitudes toward learning English and were highly motivated to study it; (2) They were more instrumentally than integratively motivated to learn English; (3) Their attitudes and motivation were positively correlated with their English proficiency. |
| Humphreys & Spratt (2008) | 526 HK college learners of different FLs | Questionnaires and interviews | (1) Affective and integrative motivation were the greatest for students learning English and the third FL, but instrumental motivation was the greatest for students learning Putonghua; (2) Significant correlation existed between effort and affective and integrative motivation. |
| Hernández (2010) | 201-semester SA college students | Questionnaires, interviews and tests | Motivation and interaction were important factors in shaping the development of speaking proficiency in the TL both at home and in SA contexts. |
| Liu (2017) | 162 (51 males, 88 females) adult learners of Chinese as a SL (SA) | Questionnaires and interviews | (1) Participants reported high integrative motivation, instrumental motivation and motivation intensity to learn Chinese, and high use of Chinese outside of class; (2) Integrative motivation was significantly positively correlated with instrumental motivation; both integrative and instrumental motivation were significantly positively correlated with motivation intensity; (3) Use of Chinese outside of class and motivation intensity were powerful predictors for self-rated competence in Chinese. |
| Phan et al. (2020) | 152 Vietnamese university students | Questionnaires and interviews | The participants were primarily extrinsically motivated and used all strategies at a medium or high level. |
| Dong et al. (2022) | 280 Chinese high school students | Questionnaires on foreign language classroom anxiety (FLCA) and expectancy-value motivation | (1) The students' FLCA demonstrated a complex relation with expectancy-value motivation: As the participants' FLCA level increased, their cost value increased, but their expectancy beliefs, intrinsic value, utility value and attainment value decreased; (2) Motivation and FLCA powerfully predicted the participants' self-rated English proficiency. |

(Continued)

| Study | Participants | Instruments | Main findings |
|---|---|---|---|
| Liu (2024) | 263 Chinese first-year undergraduate students | A mixed-form Motivational Self System Questionnaire | (1) The respondents had moderate motivation to study English; (2) They reported a significantly higher perception of their ideal L2 self and L2 learning experience than ought-to self; (3) All L2 MSSQ scales were significantly positively related to English achievement; (4) The respondents imagined themselves using English fluently and/or confidently to do/help their jobs, facilitate their study, communicate with others, do business and obtain information. |

## 6.5 Foreign language anxiety

Anxiety, originally treated as a psychological construct, refers to "the subjective feeling of tension, apprehension, nervousness, and worry associated with an arousal of the autonomic nervous system" (Spielberger, 1983: 1). It generally has three types: trait anxiety, state anxiety, and situation-specific anxiety. As a type of situation-specific anxiety, foreign language anxiety concerns "the feeling of tension and apprehension specifically associated with second language contexts, including speaking, listening, and learning" (MacIntyre & Gardner, 1994: 284). Due to the lack of uniform measures, early studies (e.g., Chastain, 1975; Kleinmann, 1977) revealed inconsistent findings of the relationship between anxiety and language learning achievements. Hence, Horwitz et al. (1986) proposed the Foreign Language Classroom Anxiety (FLCA) theory, i.e., "a distinct complex of self-perceptions, beliefs, feelings and behaviors related to classroom learning arising from the uniqueness of the language learning process" (128). They also developed a 33-item Foreign Language Classroom Anxiety Scale (FLCAS), which has been frequently used to measure foreign language classroom anxiety, and speaking anxiety in various L2 contexts (Boudreau et al., 2018). In addition to the FLCAS, researchers study foreign language anxiety via other methods like interviews, diaries, and observations. Apart from the consistently negative correlation between foreign language anxiety and L2 learning outcomes, researchers have found that students are most anxious about speaking the target language in classrooms, that foreign language anxiety is dynamic and continuously interacts with various linguistic, educational, environmental, and cultural variables such as motivation, enjoyment, and personality (e.g., Boudreau et al., 2018; Liu, 2018; Liu & Jackson, 2008; Liu & Xiangming, 2019; Shirvan & Taherian, 2021; Xiangming et al., 2020). Table 6.2 summarizes some studies on foreign language anxiety.

**Table 6.2   Example studies on foreign language anxiety**

| Study | Participants | Instruments | Main findings |
|---|---|---|---|
| Bailey (1983) | one (the researcher herself) college learner of French as a FL | Diaries | (1) The researcher was very uncomfortable and extremely anxious about the French class during the first few weeks; (2) She withdrew from the study for a while and then worked harder at some other time. |
| Gregersen & Horwitz (2002) | 4 most anxious and 4 least anxious based on FLCAS scores (college Spanish learners of English in Chile) | FLCAS and interviews | The anxious students reported higher standards for their English performance, a greater tendency toward procrastination, greater worry over the opinions of others, and a higher level of concern about their errors than the non-anxious learners, and often attributed their errors to their anxiety. |
| Ewald (2007) | 21 advanced college learners of Spanish | FLCAS and interviews | (1) Students reported experiencing anxiety in upper-level courses; (2) Teachers played a critical role in producing and reliving anxiety. |
| Liu & Jackson (2008) | 547 Chinese college EFL learners | FLCAS and other questionnaires | FLA well predicted students' performance on the oral English test and willingness to communicate (WTC) in English. |
| Gürsoy & Akin (2013) | 84 Turkish EFL learners aged 10–14 years | FLCAS and interview | (1) Younger children were less anxious than older children about FLL; (2) Examinations were the activity that caused the most anxiety for the children. |
| Dewaele & MacIntyre (2014) | 1,627 learners of English with various backgrounds | FLCAS and other questionnaires | Female participants reported significantly more FL enjoyment and FLCA than their male peers. |
| Liu (2016) | 1,160 Chinese first-year college EFL learners | Questionnaires (FL listening anxiety and strategy use) | (1) The low-proficient group was significantly more anxious about English listening and less confident in their English listening proficiency; (2) FLLA was generally significantly correlated with FLLSU for both high- and low-proficient groups. |
| Liu (2018) | 167 adult bilingual/multilingual learners of Chinese as a SL (SA) | FLCAS, other questionnaires, and interviews | (1) FLA and WTCC predicted each other and self-rated proficiency in Chinese; (2) A number of reasons were identified as responsible for FLA. |

(Continued)

| Study | Participants | Instruments | Main findings |
|---|---|---|---|
| Liu & Yuan (2021) | 182 Chinese first-year undergraduate learners of English | FLCAS and the Foreign Language Listening Anxiety (FLLA) Scale | (1) The participants experienced high levels of FLCA and FLLA both at the beginning and end of the semester, neither of which changed significantly during the semester; (2) FLCA and FLLA were highly positively related to each other; (3) FLCA and FLLA significantly predicted students' self-rated proficiency in listening and speaking English; (4) Confidence in using English, efforts and motivation to learn English, and interaction with the English teacher and peers mediated the effects of FLCA and FLLA on students' self-perceived proficiency in listening and speaking English. |
| Li & Wei (2023) | 954 Chinese middle school learners | Longitudinal: questionnaire and English achievement test | (1) Anxiety, enjoyment and boredom at T1 predicted English achievement at T2 (one week after T1) and T3 (five weeks after T1) independently, while only enjoyment predicted achievement at T4 (nine weeks after T1); (2) When combined, enjoyment was the strongest and most enduring predictor across T2–T4, followed by anxiety predicting achievement at T2–T3 negatively, while boredom completely lost its predictive power across T2–T4. |
| Liu et al. (2024) | 570 high-performing university students in China | Questionnaires on emotions and interviews | (1) The participants experienced a diversity of emotions in their English language class due to both learner-internal and external reasons, but the most often reported emotions were anxiety, enjoyment and boredom; (2) English language classroom anxiety and boredom significantly negatively predicted students' English test performance, while enjoyment significantly positively predicted the students' English test performance; (3) English language classroom anxiety debilitated English learning but motivated students to study harder as well; enjoyment facilitated English learning but students might forget much of what had been learned after class; though boredom caused some students to be absent-minded in class, most students would study on their own when feeling bored. |

# 6.6 Language learning strategy

The role of strategies in language learning has been widely acknowledged. Skehan (1989) regarded language learning strategies as one of the most important individual difference factors in L2 acquisition. Even so, considerable debate exists about how to define language learning strategies. Rubin (1987: 23) defined learning strategies as "strategies which contribute to the development of the language system which the language learner constructs and affect learning directly". Weinstein and Mayer (1986: 315) defined learning strategies as "the behaviors and thoughts that a learner engages in during learning that are intended to influence the learner's encoding process". Chamot (1987: 71) defined learning strategies as "techniques, approaches or deliberate actions that students take in order to facilitate the learning and recall of both linguistic and content area information". Oxford (1990: 8) stated that "learning strategies are specific actions taken by the learner to make learning easier, faster, more enjoyable, more self-directed, and more transferable to new situations".

Green and Oxford (1995: 262) later expanded this to be "specific actions or techniques that students use, often intentionally, to improve their progress in developing L2 skills". Of various definitions, Oxford's has been most frequently applied in empirical research.

Guided by different definitions, researchers classify strategies into different categories accordingly. For example, Ellis (1985) classified language learning strategies into three types: learning strategies, production strategies, and communication strategies. O'Malley et al. (1985) classified language learning strategies into three types: metacognitive strategies, cognitive strategies and social mediation strategies, as detailed in Table 6.3.

**Table 6.3   O'Malley et al.'s (1985) classification of strategies**

| Learning strategies | Descriptions |
| --- | --- |
| **A. Metacognitive strategies** | |
| Advance organizers | Making a preview of the organizing concept or principles in a learning activity. |
| Directed orientation | Deciding in advance what to attend to in a learning task. |
| Selective attention | Deciding in advance to attend to specific aspects of the language input or situational details in a task. |
| Self-management | Understanding and arranging for the conditions that help one learn. |
| Advance preparation | Planning for and rehearsing linguistic components necessary for a language task. |
| Self-monitoring | Correcting one's speech for accuracy or for appropriateness to context. |
| Delayed production | Consciously deciding to postpone speaking in favor of initial listening. |
| Self-evaluation | Checking learning outcomes against internal standards. |
| Self-reinforcement | Arranging rewards for successfully completing a language learning activity. |

| Learning strategies | Descriptions |
|---|---|
| **B. Cognitive strategies** | |
| Repetition | Imitating a language model, including overt practice and silent rehearsal. |
| Resourcing | Using target language reference materials. |
| Directed physical response | Relating new information to physical action as with directives. |
| Translation | Using the first language to understand and produce the second language. |
| Grouping | Reordering or reclassifying material to be learned. |
| Note-taking | Writing down main ideas, important points, outlines, or summaries of information. |
| Deduction | Conscious application of rules. |
| Recombination | Constructing language by combining known elements in a new way. |
| Imagery | Relating new information to visual concepts in memory. |
| Auditory representation | Retention of the sound or similar sound for a word, phrase, etc. |
| Keyword | Remembering a new word in the second language by mnemonic or associational techniques, e.g., keywords. |
| Contextualization | Placing a word or phrase in a meaningful language sequence. |
| Elaboration | Relating new information to existing concepts. |
| Transfer | Using previously acquired knowledge to facilitate new learning. |
| Inferencing | Using available information to guess meanings of new items, predict outcomes, etc. |
| Questions for clarification | Asking a teacher, etc. for repetition, paraphrasing, explanation, and/or examples. |
| **C. Social mediation strategies** | |
| Cooperation | Working with one or more peers to obtain feedback, pool information, etc. |

Oxford (1990) classified language learning strategies into six types: memory strategies, cognitive strategies, compensation strategies, metacognitive strategies, social strategies and affective strategies. To measure these strategies, Oxford (1990) developed the Strategy Inventory for Language Learning (SILL), which has been extensively utilized in empirical studies in various contexts. For example, Habók and Magyar (2018) used an adapted version of the SILL to examine language learning strategy use in relation to foreign language attitude, proficiency, and general school achievement among 868 lower secondary students in Years 5 and 8 in Hungary. The results showed that the students mainly used metacognitive strategies in both years and that more and less proficient language learners differed in strategy use. The study also showed that metacognitive, social, and memory strategies primarily influenced foreign language attitudes and performance in Year 5. In addition, the study demonstrated the dominant effect of metacognitive strategies and the low effect of memory strategies on foreign language attitudes and performance in Year 8.

Together with other methods such as interviews, diaries and think-aloud protocols, studies on strategy use have provided many valuable insights concerning SL/FL learning. Studies on good language learners find that more proficient language learners use more learning strategies, and more types of strategies and are more able to choose strategies appropriate to the task (O'Malley et al., 1985; Oxford, 1990; Rubin, 1987; Wenden, 1985). These studies also reveal that good language learners often seek ways to practice the L2 and maintain a conversation, have positive attitudes towards speakers of the target language, monitor their speech and that of others, seek verification and clarification, attend to both form and meaning, look for patterns, and actively participate in learning.

# Tasks

## 1. Explain the following terms.

intelligence

general intelligence

aptitude

language aptitude

attitude

motivation

language learning motivation

anxiety

foreign language anxiety

language learning strategy

## 2. Discuss the following questions.

1) How is language aptitude related to L2 learning?

2) How can learners' attitudes toward a SL/FL be measured?

3) What sorts of motivation do L2 learners have?

4) How can anxiety affect L2 learning?

5) What strategies do good language learners often use?

6) Do individual factors interact with one another? Illustrate it with an example.

## 3. Projects.

1) Find a nonnative speaker of Chinese on campus. The International Student Association is a good place to start. Interview and survey the students about their attitudes toward Chinese and motivation to study Chinese. Then write a report.

2) If you are taking a foreign language course now, keep a journal of your feelings about learning the language in class. Use the concepts learned in this unit and write a report.

3) The school administration wants to know what strategies students often use to study English and how good and poor language learners differ in their use of strategies. Please help the administration design the research and write a report.

4) Use concepts and ideas in this unit to explain why people have differential success with L2 learning.

language

culture

learning

hello

world

UNIT
7

Social-cultural factors
and second language
acquisition

# Objectives

In this unit, you will learn

—cultural factors such as language and thought, language and power, language and ideology and the Acculturation Theory;

—social factors such as social class dialect, social network, gender, restricted and elaborated codes, register, jargon and slang, pidgins, creoles, and lingua franca;

—social interactional approaches like conversation analysis and the sociocultural theory.

## 7.1  Cultural factors

Language is intrinsic to the expression of culture. Language is a fundamental aspect of cultural identity. It is the means by which we convey our innermost self from generation to generation. It is through language that we transmit and express our culture and its values.

### 7.1.1  Language and thought

A number of questions have been raised in order to determine the relationship between language and thought: Does language determine thought? Does thought determine language? How is language related to thought?

The **Sapir-Whorf hypothesis**, also known as the **Linguistic Relativity Hypothesis**, was proposed by Edward Sapir and Benjamin Lee Whorf (1956), which states that language is a shaping force and predisposes people to see the world in a certain way to guide their thinking and behavior. It proposes that language determines and influences thinking. Namely, the particular language one speaks influences the way one thinks about reality.

Two aspects are actually involved in the Sapir-Whorf hypothesis: linguistic relativity and linguistic determinism. Relativity refers to the claim that speakers are required to pay attention to different aspects of the language that are grammatically marked (e.g., articles in English or quantifiers in Chinese). Linguistic relativity claims that translating ideas from one language to another is extremely difficult and perhaps impossible. Determinism claims that our cognitive processes are influenced by the differences that are found in languages. Linguistic determinism believes that people's language dictates the way they speak.

The most famous yet the most erroneous example of the Whorf hypothesis is Whorf's observation that Eskimos have many words for snow, implying that because they live in a snowy environment, they need to come up with finer distinctions for the different types of snow. But American skiers have different words for snow, too. So the example is not as remarkable as it first may appear, because expertise leads to larger vocabularies for certain domains.

There are different versions of the hypothesis that make different claims:

- The strong version states that language determines thought and that linguistic categories limit and determine cognitive categories.

- The medium version states that language constrains thought.

- The weak version states that language and culture influence each other.

For example, there are hundreds of camel-related words in Arabic. Does this influence how an Arabic speaker thinks about camels? Clearly it does. Nevertheless, it is less clear if it is because of the various camel words that Arabic speakers think differently. It seems more plausible that the environment leads to the need for more words and expressions related to camels. Another famous example is that Hanunóo people in the Philippines have 92 different expressions for rice.

A popular topic of research relates to the number of color expressions that languages have. If the Linguistic Relativity Hypothesis were correct, color categories would be arbitrary. Different languages would "see" color differently. Yet, research shows that some cultures have only two color words (i.e., black and white) and others have three words (i.e., black, white and red). Every known language has expressions equating to black and white (dark/light). Based on the assumption that it is easier to discriminate between colors that belong to a different linguistic category, Roberson et al. (2000) studied color perception and language. The findings showed that color judgements were influenced by vocabulary.

Most people agree that there is an interaction between language and culture: Language influences, but does not determine, culture. Culture is also reflected in language. For example, in Japan, the term "uchi" (inside) and "soto" (outside) are very important for understanding Japanese culture. Everyone knows what is inside and what is outside to them. They speak of their "haha" (my/our mother) but of someone else's "okāsan" (someone else's mother). The word for mother changes depending on whose mother it is. The change is closely related to the concept of inside/outside, which is culturally determined.

### 7.1.2 Language and power

Research on the power of language suggests that language has a power of its own. This power allows a language to maintain the power behind it and create influence.

According to Ng and Deng (2017), there is power behind language and power of language, which reveals five types of relationships between language and power, as shown in

Table 7.1 (Ng & Deng, 2017: 7).

**Table 7.1    Power behind language and power of language**

| Power behind language | 1. Language reveals power. | Power of language | 1. Language maintains existing dominance. |
|---|---|---|---|
| | | | 2. Language unites and divides a nation. |
| | 2. Language reflects power. | | 3. Lan guage creates influence through words, oratories, conversations, and narratives. |

According to Ng and Deng (2017), power behind language originates from pre-existing powers behind language that it reveals and reflects and transfers the extralinguistic powers to the communication context. It exists at both micro and macro levels. At the micro level, it is the speaker's possession of a weapon, money, high social status, or other attractive personal qualities. By revealing the power in convincing language, the speaker influences the hearer. At the macro level, the power behind language is the collective power (ethnolinguistic vitality) of the communities that speak the language. For example, the use of English as a global language and international lingua franca in the contemporary world is more because of the ethnolinguistic vitality of English speakers worldwide that it reflects. The three types of power of language refer to the powers of language that are based on a language's communicative versatility and its broad range of cognitive, communicative, social, and identity functions in meaning-making, social interaction, and language policies.

Generally speaking, powerful institutions and individuals use language both as a means to construct their power and a way to maintain their power. Language thus becomes necessary for the maintenance of power, and the power of language in turn depends on the power of individuals and institutions themselves. Meanwhile, language becomes more powerful when it is understood by a wider community. Power grows when the language is used by more people for more reasons. The more powerful a language, the more independent its speakers become, and the more they can contribute to the community.

### 7.1.3  Language and ideology

Ideology is a system of mutually reinforcing beliefs, usually proposed by a group (social class) in power. An example is the Confucian ideology, a philosophy and belief system from ancient China, which focuses on the importance of having good moral character. This moral character is achieved through the virtue of "ren", or "humanity," which leads to more virtuous behaviors such as respect, altruism, and humility. Confucianism believes in ancestor worship and human-centered virtues for living a peaceful life. If the emperor has moral perfection, his rule will be peaceful and benevolent. It also stresses filial piety, or devotion to family. The worldly concern of Confucianism rests upon the belief that human beings are fundamentally good, teachable, improvable, and perfectible through personal and communal efforts, especially self-cultivation and self-creation. These ideas constitute a large part of Chinese culture.

The most perverse effect of ideology is arguably the naturalization of power imbalance: What is essentially partial and skewed point of view becomes so hidden in the ideology of discourse culture that it becomes common sense (Brown & Attardo, 2008). For example, research in racist discourse against immigrants in the British and Dutch press revealed that the most common themes in the press corresponded to the common stereotypes of racist discourse: Immigration is an invasion; immigrants are freeloaders and criminals.

Ideology manifests itself in language, as shown in Example 7.1.

### Example 7.1

(1) RIOTING BLACKS SHOT DEAD BY POLICE AS ANC LEADERS MEET

(2) POLICE SHOOT 11 DEAD IN SALISBURY RIOT

The use of the passive in Example 7.1-(1) puts the rioting blacks in evidence and deemphasizes the role of the police, while Example 7.1-(2) simply tells the truth.

#### Critical discourse analysis

Because teachers, teaching materials, and the very institutions in which they teach are steeped in the ideologically biased culture in which they operate, education perpetuates ideology. Thus, critical discourse analysis is necessary.

Critical discourse analysis is a methodology that enables a vigorous assessment of what is meant when language is used to describe and explain. The aim of critical discourse analysis is

> "to systematically explore often opaque relationships of causality and determination between a) discursive practices, events and texts, and b) wider social and cultural structures, relations and processes; to investigate how such practices, events and texts arise out of and are ideologically shaped by relations of power and struggles over power" (Fairclough, 1995: 132).

Thus, language should always be considered in relation to social contexts. The term "discourse" is used as it refers to the various ways in which people communicate through language.

### 7.1.4  Acculturation theory

The Acculturation Theory was proposed by John Schumann (1978) to describe the acquisition process of a second language by members of ethnic minorities, which typically include immigrants, migrant workers, or the children of such groups. This acquisition process takes place in natural contexts of the majority language settings (VanPatten, 2010). The core idea of the theory is that the acquisition of a second language is directly linked to the acculturation process, and that learners' success is determined by the extent to which they can orient themselves to the culture of target language (VanPatten, 2010). Schumann claims that this extent generally depends on social and psychological factors, which determine respectively the level of social distance and psychological distance L2 learner experiences in the course of learning the second language.

Social distance concerns the extent to which individual learners can identify themselves with members of the target language group and thus establish contact with them. Schumann (1978) identifies eight factors that influence social distance: social dominance, integration pattern, enclosure, cohesiveness, size, cultural congruence, attitude, and intended length of residence.

- Social dominance: The native language learners' reference group can be superior, inferior, or equal in terms of politics, culture, technology, or economics. If they view their group as superior, they may not learn the second language.

- Integration pattern: Assimilative learners give up the values and lifestyles of native language. Preservative learners retain native language values and lifestyles. Adaptive learners become bicultural and switch between groups.

- Enclosure: When groups share social facilities, enclosure is low. The more the L2 groups share social institutions such as schools, churches, workplaces, clubs, etc. with the target language group, the more favorable the conditions will be for L2 acquisition.

- Cohesiveness: Strong intra-group contact in the native language community with few contacts outside the community affects second language learning. The L2 community tends to stay as a cohesive group. But the smaller and less cohesive the L2 group, the more likely the contact with the target language group and the more favorable the conditions for L2 acquisition.

- Size: The size of the native language community can affect L2 learning. If the size of the learner's group is large, it tends to facilitate intra-group contact rather than inter-group contact.

- Congruence: The similarity and harmony between cultures impact second language learning. The more similar the culture of the two groups, the more likely it is that there will be social contact and thus language acquisition.

- Attitude: The feelings of the L2 and target language groups toward each other impact learning. The more positive the L2 group's attitudes toward the TL group, the more favorable the conditions will be for L2 learning.

- Intended length of residence: The longer L2 learners plan to stay in the L2 environment, the better for learning the target language. The length of time a learner plans to stay in the country and the permanency of residency in the country impact the motivation to learn a new language.

Thus, the large social distance between the host community and the target language speakers and culture deeply affects their acculturation, and hence their second language acquisition.

Psychological distance is the extent to which individual learners are at ease with their task of learning the target language (Schumann, 1978). Schumann (1978) identifies three factors that influence psychological distance: motivation, attitude, and culture shock.

- Motivation: The level of motivation affects learning.

- Attitude: The extent to which L2 learners view their first language as fixed and rigid impacts their learning of the target language.

- Culture shock: Feeling anxious or disoriented in the culture equates less likelihood of learning the target language.

The process of acculturation is the process of getting adapted to a new culture, which involves a new orientation of thinking and feeling on the part of an L2 learner (Brown, 1994). According to Brown (1994), as culture is an integral part of a human being, the process of acculturation takes a deeper turn when the issue of language is brought on the scene. There are five stages of acculturation:

- enthusiastic acceptance,

- doubt and reservation,

- resentment and criticism,

- adjustment,

- accommodation and evaluation.

### A. Enthusiastic acceptance

When you first arrived in the target language community, everything was new, and you were experiencing a great deal of novelty. All cultures have both good and bad characteristics. You may have been attracted to the good characteristics and overlooked the bad like alcoholism, child abuse, suicide rates, etc. It's a little bit like dating and the honeymoon. You saw only the good yet ignored the bad.

### B. Doubt and reservation

In this stage, the novelty begins to fade and you begin to realize that the target language culture is not as perfect as you thought it was upon arrival. You may have experienced what you felt like prejudice against you. What you are actually feeling is tension between the familiar and the unfamiliar. This takes its toll and you may withdraw, rather than reach out.

### C. Resentment and criticism

It is at this point that visitors to a new culture begin to see buildings as dilapidated, people as unlearned, and workers as incompetent. If you are unaware of what's happening, you may alienate those who could eventually become your friends. It might be best to think of yourself as a guest in someone else's home during this stage. How would I treat the host, even if I didn't like everything about the home setting?

### D. Adjustment

During the adjustment stage, the newcomers realize that the unhappiness and critical attitudes that they have been experiencing are due to difficulties in adjusting, rather than to deficiencies in the newfound culture. Thus, they adjust themselves accordingly to better fit the new culture.

### E. Accommodation and evaluation

During this stage, the newcomers acquire a degree of comfort in the new culture, make friends from the new culture, and begin to enjoy the experience.

## 7.2　Social factors

A dialect is a variety of a language that differs in pronunciation, grammar, or vocabulary from the standard language of the culture. An example is Cantonese of the Chinese language. A dialect is distinguished by its vocabulary, grammar, and pronunciation and by its use by a group of speakers who are geographically or socially distinct from others. For example, African American Vernacular English, also known as Black English or Ebonics, is characterized by the absence of the copula "be" (e.g., "You crazy"), multiple negation (e.g., "I don't know nobody"), and the omission of the 3rd person "-s/es" (e.g., "He like reading").

Dialect can be divided into two types: regional and social. A regional dialect is a distinct form of a language spoken in a particular geographical area. A social dialect, also known as a sociolect, is the variant of language used by a social group such as a socioeconomic class, an ethnic group, an age group, and so on. Factors that affect social dialect include social class, religion, education, profession, caste, age, and gender.

People's language reflects their social grouping when they use different social dialects. These social distinctions are also reflected in speech, and a person's social dialect reflects his/ her social background.

### 7.2.1　Social class dialect

A social class dialect is a variety of speech associated with a particular social class. More educated higher class speakers tend to use more features of the standard language, whereas the original dialect of the region is better preserved in the speech of the lower and less educated classes.

For example, standard British English, also called the Queen's English or Public School English, used to be the English of the upper classes (Dirven & Verspoor, 2004). Among older European-American speakers in Charleston, South Carolina, the absence of "r" in words such as "bear" and "court" is associated with aristocratic, high-status groups (McDavid, 1948). Labov (1969), a pioneer in the study of language and social class, investigated the pronunciation of clerks in three New York City department stores—Klein's (lower class), Macy's (middle class) and Saks' (upper-middle class). He assumed that the speech of the clerks would be representative of the speech of customers. The results showed that there was more /r/ in casual speech at Saks', and Macy's clerks were more "correct" than Saks' clerks in careful speech, though Macy's was closer to Klein's in casual speech.

This tendency of middle-class speakers to pay a lot of attention to prestige (standard) forms is called hypercorrection. Labov (1966, 1969) also studied social stratification (asking people of different social classes to read, speak, and be interviewed) and found that there were more prestige forms in careful speech and that social class had an effect on speech. The lower-middle-class participants used both standard and nonstandard forms. In the careful speech tasks, they used excessive standard forms (hypercorrection), while in casual speech they used nonstandard forms. The lower-middle class showed the greatest sensitivity or aversion to nonstandard features, even though they themselves used them. Labov explained these as examples of linguistic insecurity. He saw language change as happening through this linguistic insecurity of the lower-middle class: Hypercorrection leads to the spread of prestige forms throughout the speech community.

In the 1950s in England, many pairs of words placed the speaker either in the "upper-class speakers" or the "non-upper-class speakers", as shown in Example 7.2.

### *Example 7.2*

| **Upper-class speaker** | **Non-upper-class speaker** |
| --- | --- |
| sitting room | lounge |

| lavatory | toilet |
| --- | --- |
| sofa | settee |

Caste is another type of social stratification. In a caste-based society, social position is inherited and fixed throughout life. Caste-based societies often assign different lexical items and grammatical structures to a given caste. The Kirundi and Burundi (Central Africa) have a caste system in which seniority and gender are important: When people meet, the older person speaks first, the male first. In Indonesia, the Javanese language reflects social status not only in the choice of linguistic forms but also in the combination of forms used by each social group.

### 7.2.2 Social network

A social network is a social structure made up of a set of social actors (e.g., individuals, groups, organizations, or even entire societies), sets of dyadic ties, and other social interactions between the actors. Social networks are clustered around kinship, occupation, education, and group membership. These are frequently multi-complex networks in which one person plays multiple roles. Thus, people are constantly constructing their identities. It is not that people are essentially working class or middle class, but that they collectively decide what it means to speak like a person from the working class or middle class. Networks reinforce these largely unconscious decisions.

### 7.2.3 Gender

The norms of appropriate ways of talking for different genders are an example of the concept of power in language (Weatherall, 2002). Language is a complex and dynamic system that produces meaning about social categories such as gender.

The notion of gender varies from culture to culture and from time to time. As femininity and masculinity are not fixed concepts, their style of talking can also be a result of power relations in society that regulate social standards. For example, there is no equivalent for "sir" when addressing a female authority, which is not related to the language itself but to the perception that authorities have always been male. Another example is the way in which women are addressed as "Miss", "Mrs.", or "Ms.", while men are only addressed as "Mr.", which is a term that shows their gender not marital status. Unlike men, women's relationships can affect their social status, based on which they are judged and qualified.

Robin Lakoff (1975) identified a "women's register", which she argued serves to maintain women's (inferior) role in society. Lakoff argued that women tend to use linguistic forms that reflect and reinforce a subordinate role. These include tag questions, question intonation, and weak directives. Aubrey and Harrison (2004) identified gender stereotypes in children's television programs and evaluated the effects of these stereotypes on children's personal gender-role values and interpersonal attraction. The study found that male characters were more likely to ask questions, assert opinions, and direct others than female characters, while female characters were more likely to "receive or make comments about body or beauty" than their male counterparts. As found in Mulac et al. (1985), the following tend to be higher in frequency for males: vocalized pauses, action verbs, present tense verbs, justifiers, subordinating conjunctions, and grammatical errors. Yet, the following occur more for females: total verbs, uncertainty verbs, adverbials beginning sentences, judgmental adjectives, concrete nouns, and polite forms. Meanwhile, research shows that men generally use minimal responses (i.e., paralinguistic features such as "mm" and "yeah") and questions less frequently (Todd, 1993; Zimmerman & West, 1975) and change subjects more frequently than women (Dorval, 1990).

Some natural languages have intricate systems of gender-specific vocabulary. For example, Irish Sign Language developed separate male and female vocabularies as a result of single-sex schools for the deaf, which can still be seen today. The indigenous Australian language Yanyuwa has separate dialects for men and women.

### 7.2.4 Restricted and elaborated codes

Code refers to a set of organizing principles behind the language employed by members of a social group (Littlejohn, 2002).

The construct of restricted and elaborated language codes was introduced by Bernstein in the 1960s (Chandler, 2004). Bernstein proposed a sociolinguistic theory of language codes in which there are elaborated and restricted codes within the broader category of language codes (Clark, 2013).

The **restricted code** is suitable for insiders who share assumptions and understanding on the topic, whereas the elaborated code does not assume that the listener shares these assumptions or understandings, and thus the elaborated code is more explicit, more thorough, and does not require the listener to read between the lines.

According to Atherton (2002), the restricted code works better than the elaborated code in situations where there is a great deal of shared and taken-for-granted knowledge in the group of speakers. It is economical and rich, conveying a vast amount of meaning with a few words, each of which has a complex set of connotations and acts like an index, pointing the listener to much more information which remains unsaid. Within the restricted code, speakers draw on background knowledge and shared understanding. This type of code creates a sense of inclusion, a feeling of belonging to a certain group. Restricted codes can be found among friends and families, and other intimately knit groups.

According to Atherton (2002), the **elaborated code** explains everything, not because it is better but because it is necessary for everyone to understand. The elaborated code works well in situations where there is no prior or shared understanding and knowledge, where a more thorough explanation is required. If one is saying something new to someone they've never met before, they would most certainly communicate in the elaborated code. Explicitness is valued. But elaborated code speakers also use the restricted code in situations of intimacy or familiarity.

The elaborated code can stand on its own, and is complete and full of detail. Most people overhearing a conversation would be able to understand it. However, the restricted code is shorter, more condensed, and requires background information and prior knowledge. A person overhearing a conversation full of restricted code would be quite lost. It would be easily identifiable as an insider's conversation. According to Bernstein (1971: 135), "Clearly one code is not better than another; each possesses its own aesthetic, its own possibilities. Society, however, may place different values on the orders of experience elicited, maintained and progressively strengthened through the different coding systems".

Bernstein suggests a correlation between social class and the use of either elaborated or restricted codes. He argues that working class people use the restricted code, while middle-class people use both restricted and elaborated codes. This is because the middle class, being more geographically, socially, and culturally mobile, has access to both restricted and elaborated codes (Atherton, 2002). The restricted code is less formal, with shorter phrases inserted in the middle or at the end of a thought to confirm understanding. For example, "you know", "you know what I mean", "right?" and "don't you think?". Elaborated codes have a longer, more complicated sentence structure that uses unusual words and thoughts.

### 7.2.5 Register

The term "register" was first used by Reid (1956), and was popularized in the 1960s by a group of linguists who wanted to distinguish between variations in language according to the user (defined by variables such as social background, geography, gender and age), and variations according to use, in the sense that each speaker has a range of varieties and choices among them at different times (Halliday, 1964). The focus is on the way in which language is used for certain subject matters in particular situations, such as the language of a biology research lab, a news report, or a bedroom. For example, when speaking officially or in a public setting, an English speaker may be more likely to follow prescriptive norms for formal usage.

Register often refers to the degree of formality of language (Trudgill, 1992). In a more general sense, it refers to the language used by a group of people who share similar work or interests, such as doctors or lawyers. For example, "Would you mind passing the salt?" is appropriate for a formal situation with strangers, while "Pass me the salt" is often used for a situation where friends are talking.

The concept of register is also often defined as "related" to contextual factors, because among the various parameters that have been proposed as determining register are:

- Subject matter: What the text is about and what the speakers are talking about will determine, to a certain extent, their choices at various linguistic levels (e.g., lexical and syntactic levels). Chemistry, physics, or language have their own registers.

- Social roles/situations: Who the speaker is and what he/she does.

- Discursive function: What the speaker is using the text for, such as to discuss and to insult.

Joos (1961) distinguishes five styles based primarily on the roles of the speaker and listener, the situation, and the purposes of the exchange. Linguistic features follow from these constraints:

- Frozen: Also referred as static register. At this level, language is literally "frozen" in time and form. It does not change. This type of language is often learned and repeated by rote such as biblical quotations, prayers, etc. The wording is exactly the same each time it is spoken.

- Formal: This style is impersonal and formal. The speaker/writer uses complete sentences, avoids slang and may use technical or academic vocabulary (e.g., "do not" instead of "don't"). This is the register used for most academic and scientific publishing. At this level, it is one-way communication, with no interruptions.

- Consultative: This is the register used when consulting an expert, such as a doctor or a teacher. This is a standard form of communication, with possible interruptions. The language used is more precise and professional.

- Casual: This register is conversational in tone. It is the language used among and between peers, friends and acquaintances. The language is informal, with slang, colloquialisms, ellipses, and frequent interruptions.

- Intimate: This is the most intimate form of language and thus most common among family members and close friends. It is best avoided in public and professional situations. This register may include private vocabulary and nonverbal messages. Intonation is more important than wording or grammar.

Knowing what the various registers are, how to differentiate between them, and when to use which one increases the chances of being accepted by groups and speakers in a variety of contexts.

### 7.2.6    Jargon and slang

Both jargon and slang are two special types of language varieties. The main difference between jargon and slang is that **jargon** is a terminology that is used in relation to a specific activity, profession, group, or event, whereas **slang** is the use of informal words and expressions that are not considered standard in the speaker's dialect or language.

Jargon is the specialized, often technical, language that is used by people in a particular field, profession, or social group. They are special words or expressions that belong to a specific profession or activity. It is the terminology of science, technology, trade, art, etc. The people outside that particular field will not understand the meanings of these words. Jargons have two main functions: a) to provide speakers of specialized domains with clear, unambiguous terms to refer to their activities, and b) to provide speakers of a subgroup with a means of marking in-group membership and excluding outsiders.

The following are some specific fields and jargon used in them.

**A. Police jargon**

*Code Eight:* Term that means the officer needs help immediately.

*FTP:* The failure of an individual to pay a fine.

*Suspect:* A person whom the police think may have committed a crime.

**B. Engineering jargon**

*CADD:* Computer aided drafting and design.

*QFD:* Quality Function Deployment.

*Stochastic:* Statistically random variation.

**C. Business jargon**

*Bang for the buck:* To get the most for your money.

*Open the kimono:* To share information with an outside party.

*Sweat equity:* To get a stake in the business instead of money.

Over time, some jargon can become accepted words and understood by a larger group of people. For example, words like "RAM", "byte", and "hexadecimal", which were computing science jargon, are known by everyone.

Slang is the informal language of conversations, text messages, and other casual social communication among friends. It is always used by people who share similar social backgrounds and age groups, often younger or "less respectable" than the majority, and is based on a very informal or very innovative lexicon that often replaces other words available in the general lexicon (Brown & Attardo, 2008).

A special feature of slang is that slang words do not stay in the language for long. Many slang words disappear, and new words come into the language. For example, now it is very "uncool" to use the words "hip", "groovy", or "dough", but it is not always the case. There are some words that were introduced into the language as slang but have evolved into standard words, such as "taxi", "bogus", "hoax", and "skyscraper".

A new slang word can come into being in two ways: A new word can be coined or invented, or an old word can be given a new meaning. For example, the word "wicked" originally means "cruel" or "evil", but in slang "wicked" means "wonderful" or "excellent". Table 7.2 shows both the similarities and distinctions between jargon and slang.

**Table 7.2　Differences between jargon and slang**

| Jargon | Slang |
| --- | --- |
| Both are a way of communicating within special groups of individuals who understand the actual meaning behind words or phrases. | |
| A particular variety of language used in a specific profession or activity. | A colloquial variety of language used in highly informal situations. |
| Can be used in both written and spoken contexts. | Used in spoken language only. |
| Not informal. | Informal. |
| Can be used in a professional context. | Cannot be used in a professional context. |

### 7.2.7　Pidgin, creole and lingua franca

A **pidgin** is a language that comes about as a result of contact between two groups who speak different languages and do not understand each other. It has no native speakers. It is often based on a simplified version of a main language, while borrowing vocabulary and grammar from several additional languages. For example, the original lingua franca used around the Mediterranean was a pidgin language: It was based on simplified Italian, with additions from Greek, French, Arabic, and others.

In order to create a pidgin, there must be regular contact between people speaking different languages, there needs to be a reason for communication (such as trade), and there should be a lack of another easily accessible language between the two parties. Pidgins have a distinct set of characteristics that distinguish them from the first and second languages spoken by the pidgin developers. Features of pidgins include:

- simple grammar (lack of conjugation, tenses, cases, etc.),
- simple phonology,

- limited vocabulary,

- a large number of polysemous words,

- words can function as nouns, adjectives, adverbs, or verbs,

- few prepositions, and

- no writing system.

Pidgins are used in contact situations. If they are no longer useful, they die. If they are useful, they become a lingua franca and in the process become nativized (acquire native speakers) and become creoles.

A **creole** is a pidgin that has become the first language of a new generation of speakers (Wardhaugh, 2006). Creoles have their own vocabulary, distinct from their origin languages, and a fully developed system of grammar. An example of a creole is Swahili, which grew out of Arabic and Bantu languages of East Africa. The Bazaar Malay language spoken in Malaysia is another example. Creoles differ from pidgins in that creoles have been nativized by children as their primary languages, so they have features of natural language that are normally missing from pidgins.

A **lingua franca** is a language used for communication between people who do not share a common native language. Generally, a lingua franca is a third language that is distinct from the native languages of both parties involved in the communication. Sometimes, as the language becomes more widespread, the native populations of an area will speak the lingua franca to each other as well. It is distinct from a pidgin in that members of the same populations rarely use the pidgin to talk to one another.

Lingua franca essentially means "language of commerce", helping to facilitate trade and cultural exchange. For this reason, lingua francas are also called "trade" or "bridge" languages. Throughout history and in various places around the globe, various languages have been used as lingua francas: Greek was used in the heyday of the Hellenistic influence, Latin during the Roman Empire, Aramaic in Western Asia, and today, French, Urdu, and Swahili are used as lingua francas in certain parts of the world. Today, lingua francas play an important role in global communication as well. The United Nations defines its official languages as Arabic, Chinese, English, French, Russian, and Spanish. The official language of international air traffic control is English, while multilingual areas like Asia and Africa define several unofficial lingua francas to facilitate easier communication between ethnic groups and regions.

A lingua franca is defined by its function, which is to communicate between people who are not born speaking the same language. Creole and pidgin, on the other hand, are defined by their origins and by the populations that use them. Pidgin is a new language created from two existing languages as its speakers do not speak a common language, whereas lingua franca is an already existing language that is spoken by all parties involved. Although quite often many pidgin and creole languages can function as lingua francas, lingua francas themselves most often are neither pidgins nor creoles. Table 7.3 indicates their general features and differences.

**Table 7.3  Features of pidgin, creole and lingua franca**

|  | Pidgin | Creole | Lingua franca |
|---|---|---|---|
| Definition | A language developed from a mixture of two languages and used as a way of communicating between people who do not share a common language. | A language developed out of a pidgin. | A language used for communication between people who speak different languages. |
| Native language |  | A native language of a particular community. | Maybe a native language of a particular community. |
| Language features | A simplified language. |  | Not necessarily a simplified language. |
| Special features | Create a new language from two existing languages. |  | Use an already existing language that is spoken by all parties involved. |
| Examples | Hawaiian pidgin English |  | Latin, English, Chinese |

## (7.3) Social-interactional approaches

According to sociolinguistics, learning is linked to social and local ecology: It is adaptive to an emergent set of resources that are embodied in social interactions. Linguistic utterances are sensitive to and dependent upon their interactional contexts. With a social interactive perspective on language, the linguistic code cannot be understood as an isolated phenomenon outside of its social context. Nor can one understand how learning takes place without the support of the social context. Isolated grammaticality judgments or experiments of psycholinguistic processing make little sense within this paradigm.

### 7.3.1  Conversation analysis

According to Sacks (1995), conversations are structurally organized phenomena which have some kind of order. Conversation analysis (CA) is an approach to the study of orders of talk-in-interactions that take place with any individual and in any setting, embracing both verbal and nonverbal conduct. It does not study the structure of language that is used but rather focuses on how language is used in the form of requests, complaints, proposals, or accusations. It aims to discover how participants understand and respond to one another in their conversational turns, with a central focus on how sequences of action are generated (Schegloff, 1992).

The data used in CA take the form of video- or audio-recorded conversations, collected with or without researchers' involvement, typically from a video camera or other recording device in the space where the conversation takes place (e.g., a living room, a picnic, or a doctor's office). The researchers construct detailed transcriptions from the recordings, containing as much detail as possible (Sidnell, 2016). This transcription often contains additional information about nonverbal communication and the way in which people say things. After transcription, researchers conduct inductive data-driven analysis, aiming to find recurring patterns of interaction. Based on the analysis, the researchers identify regularities, rules or models to describe these patterns, enhancing, modifying or replacing initial hypotheses.

A conversation is viewed as a collection of turns of speaking, in which errors or misunderstandings in speech are addressed with repairs, and turns may be marked by the delay between them or by other linguistic features.

- Turn-taking: A process by which interactants allocate the right or obligation to participate in an interactional activity (Sacks et al., 1974).

### Example 7.3

Salesman: This is your size. Try it on.

Customer: OK, thanks.

- Repair: The mechanisms through which certain problems in interactions are handled. Repair segments are classified by who initiates the repair (self or other), by who resolves the problem (self or other), and by how it unfolds within a turn or sequence of turns (Schegloff et al., 1977).

### 7.3.2 Sociocultural theory

The sociocultural theory is based on the work by the Russian psychologist Vygotsky (1978), who considered the important contributions that society makes to individual development. This theory stresses the interaction between developing individuals and the culture in which they live. According to Vygotsky, children are born with basic biological constraints on their minds. Each culture, however, provides "tools of intellectual adaptation". These tools allow children to use their abilities in a way that is adaptive to the culture in which they live. For example, while one culture might emphasize memory strategies such as note-taking, another might use tools like reminders or rote memorization.

The sociocultural theory views human development as a socially mediated process in which children acquire their cultural values, beliefs, and problem-solving strategies through collaborative dialogues with more knowledgeable members of society. There are a number of important concepts in this theory: mediation, regulation, internalization, and the zone of proximal development.

Mediation is the most important of the concepts, because sociocultural theory assumes that human activity (including cognitive activity) is mediated by what are known as symbolic artifacts (higher-level cultural tools), such as language and literacy, and by material artifacts. These artifacts mediate the relationship between human beings and the social and material world around us.

Within sociocultural theory, we humans use symbols as tools to mediate psychological activity and control our psychological processes. This control is voluntary and allows us to attend to certain things, to plan, and to think rationally. The primary tool we use is language, which allows us to be connected to our environments (both physical and social). Language gives us humans the power to go beyond the immediate environment and to think and talk about events and objects that are distinct both physically and temporally.

Regulation is a form of mediation. As children learn language, they also learn to regulate their activities linguistically. There are three stages in the development of self-regulation. The first stage involves the use of objects as a way of thinking (object-regulation). For example, parents use objects like sticks to help children with the abstract concept of counting. The second stage is known as other regulation whereby learning is regulated by others rather than objects. Then comes self-regulation when activities can be performed with little or no external support. This occurs through the internalization of information, such as addition or subtraction without the use of sticks.

Internalization is the process that allows humans to transfer the relationship between an individual and his/her environment to later performance. Imitation can lead to internalization, which can be both immediate, intentional, and delayed, as seen in early child language acquisition and beginners' learning of a second language. The items that learners focus on in these imitation situations are controlled by the learner and not necessarily by the teacher's agenda.

The zone of proximal development is "the distance between the actual developmental level as determined by independent problem solving and the level of potential development as determined through problem-solving under adult guidance or in collaboration with more capable peers" (Vygotsky, 1978: 86). This means that learning results from interpersonal activity and that it is interpersonal activity that forms the basis of individual functioning. This clearly embodies the social nature of learning and underscores the importance of collaborative learning as it shapes what is learned. As children are allowed to stretch their skills and knowledge, often by observing someone who is slightly more advanced than themselves, they are able to progressively expand this zone of proximal development. For example, a child who could not solve the jigsaw puzzle by himself and would have taken a long time to do so, was able to solve it after interacting with his father. Eventually, he developed competence in this skill that would be applied to future jigsaws.

The sociocultural theory believes that everything is learned on two levels: first, through interaction with others, and then integrated into the individual's mental structure (Vygotsky, 1978). Every function in the child's cultural development appears twice: a) first on the social level, and later on the individual level, b) first between people (interpsychological), and then within the child (intrapsychological). This applies equally to voluntary attention, to logical memory, and to the formation of concepts. All higher functions originate as actual relationships between individuals.

# Tasks

## 1. Explain the following terms.

| | | |
|---|---|---|
| Sapir Whorf hypothesis | ideology | critical discourse analysis |
| Acculturation Theory | enthusiastic acceptance | doubt and reservation |
| resentment and criticism | adjustment | accommodation and evaluation |
| social class dialect | restricted code | elaborated code |
| register | jargon | slang |
| pidgin | creole | lingua franca |
| dialect | conversation analysis | sociocultural theory |

## 2. Read the following statements and decide whether they are true (√) or false (x).

1) Linguistic relativity claims that a person's language determines his/her thought. (   )

2) Language itself has no power but is endowed power by its users. (   )

3) Language reflects ideology. (   )

4) Adaptive learners benefit from the acculturation process more than assimilative learners. (   )

5) Strong intra-group contact in the native language community facilitates the acquisition of a second language. (    )

6) Learners go through different stages of acculturation at similar speeds. (    )

7) A lingua franca is a newly created language for communication. (    )

8) Communication can be (more) successful if a person knows how to switch between registers in different situations. (    )

## 3. Discuss the following questions.

1) What is social distance? What factors affect social distance?

2) What is psychological distance? What factors affect psychological distance?

3) What do learners experience during the process of acculturation? What would happen if their experiences are not good during the process?

4) What are the similarities and differences among pidgin, creole and lingua franca?

5) How is gender related to language? What are the features of male and female language?

6) What is formal style? When is it often used?

7) When do people use the restricted code?

8) What is the zone of proximal development? How can it be applied to classroom teaching and learning?

9) Why is hypercorrection important?

10) How does studying people in networks differ from studying people in classes?

## 4. Projects.

1) Quite many studies show that around one third of Chinese university students are quiet/ unwilling to speak English in English language class. Please account for this from linguistic, educational, and sociocultural perspectives. Illustrate your ideas with examples.

2) As an international lingua franca, different English varieties exist in this world: American English, British English, Australian English, Hong Kong English, Singaporean English, etc. Please design a study to explore learners' perceptions of different varieties of English and explain the results from socio-cultural perspectives.

3) List 3–5 taboo words in the Chinese culture and explain why they are taboo words. Are they always taboo words? Why? Are they taboos in all situations? Why? For all speakers? Why? Explain with examples.

language

culture

learning

hello

world

**UNIT**

**8**

# Topics and types of data in second language acquisition

# Objectives

In this unit, you will learn

—some example research topics;

—different types of data and data collection methods;

—strategies to analyze data.

## 8.1 Research topics

Second language acquisition (SLA) research involves a multitude of topics on all aspects of L2 teaching and learning. The following are some example topics:

- early developments in SLA research;

- Krashen's Input Hypothesis;

- developments in theories on L2 motivation;

- the role of instruction in L2 acquisition of grammar;

- L2 acquisition of phonology;

- the innate approach to language acquisition;

- L2 acquisition of vocabulary;

- L2 and Universal Grammar;

- bilingual cognition and language teaching;

- university students' use of English learning strategies;

- students' willingness to communicate in Chinese as an L2;

- cohesive devices used in Chinese learners' English compositions;

- features of utterances produced by beginning learners of English;

- code-switching and code-mixing in conversations among L2 learners;

- transfer from L1 to L2;

- age and second language learning outcomes;

- L2 writing anxiety;

- effects of feedback on L2 writing.

## 8.2　Types of data

Data in SLA research can be naturally observed, elicited under controlled observation, or experimentally elicited through controlled procedures (Bennett-Kastor, 1988; Chaudron, 2003). Of the naturally observed data sources, there are three types: "Indirect or anecdotal evidence; native speaker 'intuitions', especially as judgments of the acceptability of utterances; and 'raw' data actually manifested in conversational and other naturally occurring forms." (Bennett-Kastor, 1988: 26)

Data are often collected by certain methods which are used to elicit, observe and record language and language-related behaviors of L2 learners, and to enable interpretations about: a) a learner's linguistic system, like the underlying mental representations of the L2, b) the development or change in a learner's linguistic system, and c) factors that may facilitate or hinder a learner's development towards the target L2 (Norris & Ortega, 2003).

**Table 8.1　Types of data and data collection methods** (Chaudron, 2003: 764)

| Naturalistic (contextualized) | Elicited production | Experimental (decontextualized) |
|---|---|---|
| Learner speech production | | |
| ▲ Recorded natural (spontaneous) speech | Role-play | Online processing measures (sentence matching/verification, |
|     **Communication task** | (meaning-focused) | signal detection, word |
| | Story (video) retelling | recognition, decision) |
| Unstructured interviews | Structured interviews | |
| | | Utterance completion |
| | Picture description/picture prompts | Elicited imitation |
| | Instruction giving | |
| Classroom observation | Discourse completion | Word association |
| | | Elicited translation |
| | | Sentence manipulation |
|     **Communication task** | (structure-focused) | |
| | Structured questionnaire | |
| | OPI | |
| | SOPI | Discrete point tests |
| | Stimulated recall | Metalinguistic tests |
| | (verbal reports, etc.) | (card sorting, grammaticality |
| Diary (self) | Integrated (e.g., cloze) tests | judgments, magnitude scaling, |
| | | paired comparisons, |
| ▼ Observational notes | | sentence correction, |
| Reflection on production: | | rule expression) |
|   Perception/interpretation | | |

### 8.2.1 Naturalistic data

An important method of collecting naturalistic data is naturalistic observation. In order to provide adequate evidence to describe, interpret, and explain an event, observation must be systematic, including details of the physical and verbal context in which observations and recordings are made.

The advantages of data collected via naturalistic observation are that it truly reflects L2 learner's speech or behavior in the target language, and that very large amounts of learner production data can be collected.

Classroom observation is a special case of naturalistic observation. Classroom observation generally aims to serve three purposes: a) to improve student outcomes by improving the instructional prowess of the teacher; b) to investigate possible inequities in instruction among different groups of students; and c) to provide researchers with information on current educational practices and to identify instructional problems.

There are different ways for conducting classroom observation, such as homegrown in-house methods and nationally standardized models. Checklists, charts, rating scales, narrative descriptions, and interactive coding systems are examples of effective observational techniques. Good classroom observation often contains most or all of the following elements:

- a stated purpose for the observation;
- a specific observational focus;
- operational definitions of all the observed behaviors;
- training procedures for observers;
- an observation schedule;
- a setting;
- a unit of time;
- a method to record the data;
- a method to process and analyze data.

A classroom observation can be as brief as a few minutes or as long as an entire school day or more. It has been used to analyze teacher behavior, classroom interaction, vocabulary awareness, classroom participation, and so on. For example, Adams (1978) kept a systematic record of Spanish-speaking ESL (English as a second language) learners' production of a variety of morphemes and syntactic structures over a two-year period. These results were compared with elicited imitation and translation tasks involving similar structures. Liu (2009) observed Chinese EFL (English as a foreign language) students' classroom participation for seven consecutive weeks to examine their willingness to communicate in English.

### 8.2.2  Elicited data

#### 8.2.2.1  (Un)Structured interviews

Interviews involve social interactions. Researchers can ask different types of questions, which generate different types of data accordingly. For example, closed questions provide people with a fixed set of responses, whereas open questions allow people to express what they think in their own words.

Interviews take many forms: formal, informal, structured, and unstructured. A structured interview is used when the interviewer reads out a set of prepared questions. It has a standardized format, which means that the same questions are asked to each interviewee in the same order. The interviewer does not deviate from the interview schedule (except to clarify the meaning of the question) or probe beyond the answers received.

Structured interviews are easy to replicate as a fixed set of closed questions are used. They are quick to conduct, which means that many interviews can take place within a short amount of time. Nevertheless, structured interviews are not flexible and may overlook much information, as only prepared questions are asked.

Unstructured interviews include not only prepared questions but also relevant questions arising from the interactions (mainly interviewees' answers). Meanwhile, the interviewer may modify the prepared questions to suit the interviewees' specific experiences. Consequently, unstructured interviews are more flexible and generate richer data. Understandably, it is more time-consuming to conduct an unstructured interview and analyze the generated data.

Interviews are often recorded by the interviewer, and the data are written up as transcripts (written accounts of interview questions and answers), which will be analyzed at a later date. Interviews can be used to generate data with a specific focus such as word order and negation, past time reference, lexical development, subject/topic prominence, tense and aspect, speech acts, pragmatics, background information, feelings, attitudes, perceptions, ratings, and strategy use (see Table 8.2).

**Table 8.2   Sample interview questions**

| Focus | Examples of questions and probes |
| --- | --- |
| Introduction | Good afternoon! I'm Eddy. What's your name? |
| Background information | How long have you studied English?<br>How do you usually study English? (e.g., at school, have private English tutors, take English lessons outside?) |

(Continued)

| Focus | Examples of questions and probes |
|---|---|
| Motivation to study English | Why do you study English? (e.g., school requirements, to get high scores, etc.) Are there other reasons to study English? |
| Perceptions of culture | What did you think of Chinese people before you came to China? What do you think of them now? Are there any differences between your perceptions? Why? |
| Ending | Well, all questions have been asked. Thank you very much! |

#### 8.2.2.2 Communication tasks

Communication tasks vary considerably, from map reading, real-world sales exchanges, information-getting tasks, and problem-solving discussions, to narrower tasks such as searching for differences in pictures, describing images, or sorting unordered picture sequences. They can be used to examine effects of interaction on SLA or L2 acquisition/use.

#### 8.2.2.3 Story-retelling

Retelling involves students orally reconstructing a story that has been presented to them in either written, picture, audio, or video mode. It is used to investigate morphological features, L2 lexical development, anaphoric reference, and topic- or subject-prominence.

#### 8.2.2.4 Role plays and discourse completion

Role plays and discourse completion tests (DCTs) have been used predominantly in SLA research to elicit data on pragmatic abilities in a variety of speech acts, such as requests and apologies. A DCT consists of a one-sided role play containing a situational prompt that one participant reads to elicit the responses of another participant.

Role plays are used to elicit data that more closely resembles naturally occurring speech acts; DCTs often produce data between naturally occurring speech and scripted speech acts.

#### 8.2.2.5 (Simulated) oral proficiency interview

The ACTFL (American Council on the Teaching of Foreign Languages) Oral Proficiency Interview (OPI) is a valid and reliable means of assessing how well a person speaks a language. The OPI is proficiency-based and assesses the ability to use language effectively and appropriately in real-life situations.

The OPI is a 20–30-minute one-on-one interview between a certified ACTFL tester and an examinee. The tester adjusts his/her approach to the OPI based on the evidence of proficiency that he/she is able to identify in the test taker's performance. The OPI is a criterion-referenced assessment. The speaker's performance is compared to the criteria outlined in the *ACTFL Proficiency Guidelines.*

The OPI has four parts: a) Introduction, in which the tester confirms the test taker's identity; b) Warm-up, in which the OPI tester initiates a discussion of some general topics to gain an initial impression of the test taker's speaking ability; c) Interview, which contains two types of approaches to questions—level checks and probes. Level checks explore the highest proficiency level at which a test taker can function consistently. Probes explore a level above the level checks in order to gather evidence of the level at which the speaker can no longer sustain performance. The tester must elicit evidence of linguistic breakdown in order to determine the proficiency level. The tester moves between level checks and probes in order to arrive at the final rating; d) The last part is cool-down, in which the tester asks a few questions to bring the conversation back to tasks that a test taker can easily perform, and then ends the interview.

The Simulated Oral Proficiency Interview (SOPI) is a performance-based, tape-mediated speaking test. It follows the general structure of the Oral Proficiency Interview (OPI) and relies on audio-taped instructions and a test booklet to elicit language from the examinee. Unlike many semi-direct tests, the SOPI contextualizes all tasks to ensure that they appear as authentic as possible.

The prototypical SOPI follows the same four phases as the OPI: warm-up, level checks, probes, and cool-down. The prototypical SOPI includes picture-based tasks that allow examinees to perform tasks such as asking questions, giving directions based on a simple map, describing a place, or narrating a sequence of events based on the illustrations provided. Other SOPI tasks require examinees to talk about selected topics or perform in real-life situations. These tasks assess the examinee's ability to manage functions at the advanced and superior levels, including apologizing, describing a process, supporting an opinion, and speaking persuasively.

Because the SOPI format is flexible, it is often tailored to the desired level of examinee proficiency and to specific examinee age groups, backgrounds, and professions. It has been used by various institutions to develop tests to meet their specific needs. For example, Stanford University uses the SOPI to diagnose and place students in foreign language classes.

### 8.2.2.6 Stimulated recall

Stimulated recall, also known as think-aloud (protocols), introspective/retrospective interviews, verbal reports, and cued recall, is a method used to elicit from L2 subjects, not a direct linguistic performance, but a more reflective, metalinguistic analysis or description of their language use, and internal representations or reconstructions of what they have said/ done and how they arrived at their performance. It has been used to elicit learners' awareness and explanations of such phenomena as their tense and aspect use, general grammar rule awareness and correction, vocabulary knowledge, and decoding or writing processes.

### 8.2.3　Experimental data

#### 8.2.3.1　Decision tasks

Decision tasks ask learners to make decisions among options (categories, pictures, sentences, multiple choices, preferences for appropriateness, referents, and so on). A good example is sentence-matching, which involves a time-controlled presentation of two sentences (simultaneously or sequentially), with the learner having to decide whether the two are the same or different. Another good example is survey, which asks participants to choose the best response from several options for each survey item.

Decision tasks have been used to examine phrasal verbs, anaphora, reflexives, object pronouns, verb tense/aspect, strategy use, motivation, attitudes, perceptions, and so on.

**Table 8.3　A sample questionnaire**

| English Speaking Anxiety Scale items (Liu, 2018) | SD | D | N | A | SA |
|---|---|---|---|---|---|
| 1. I never feel quite sure of myself when I am speaking English in my class. | 1 | 2 | 3 | 4 | 5 |
| 2. I don't worry about making mistakes in the English class. | 1 | 2 | 3 | 4 | 5 |
| 3. It frightens me when I don't understand what the teacher is saying in English. | 1 | 2 | 3 | 4 | 5 |
| 4. I start to panic when I have to speak without preparation in the English class. | 1 | 2 | 3 | 4 | 5 |
| 5. It embarrasses me to volunteer answers in my English class. | 1 | 2 | 3 | 4 | 5 |
| 6. I feel confident when I speak English in class. | 1 | 2 | 3 | 4 | 5 |
| 7. I am afraid that my English teacher is ready to correct every mistake I make. | 1 | 2 | 3 | 4 | 5 |
| 8. I can feel my heart pounding when I'm going to be called on in the English class. | 1 | 2 | 3 | 4 | 5 |
| 9. I always feel that the other students speak English better than I do. | 1 | 2 | 3 | 4 | 5 |
| 10. I feel very self-conscious about speaking English in front of other students. | 1 | 2 | 3 | 4 | 5 |
| 11. I get nervous and confused when I am speaking English in class. | 1 | 2 | 3 | 4 | 5 |
| 12. I get nervous when I don't understand every word the English teacher says. | 1 | 2 | 3 | 4 | 5 |
| 13. I am afraid that the other students will laugh at me when I speak English. | 1 | 2 | 3 | 4 | 5 |
| 14. I get nervous when the English teacher asks questions which I haven't prepared in advance. | 1 | 2 | 3 | 4 | 5 |
| 15. I'm afraid to give wrong answers in my English class. | 1 | 2 | 3 | 4 | 5 |

(SD = strongly disagree = 1; D = disagree = 2; N = neither disagree nor agree = 3; A = agree = 4; SA = strongly agree = 5)

### 8.2.3.2   Elicited production

Elicited production is used to reveal L2 learners' grammar by having them produce particular sentence structures. The syntactic structures of interest are elicited in the broader context of picture stimuli, questions, or other prompts, as shown in Example 8.1.

### *Example 8.1*

Experimenter: In this story, the teacher is punishing one of the students. Ask which one.

Learner: Which student is getting punished by the teacher?

The elicited production technique enables the experimenter to control the meaning that is to be associated with the targeted utterance and to evoke sentences corresponding to complex syntactic structures. This technique has been utilized to explore L2 learners' ability to create new linguistic forms and syntactic development.

### 8.2.3.3   Elicited imitation

Elicited imitation is a language sampling procedure in which a learner is asked to accurately repeat an utterance that illustrates some grammatical or lexical feature. In most clinical applications of this technique, the stimulus sentences are presented without any relevant context or clarification. The assumption is that success in exact imitation demonstrates the learner's possession of the grammatical or lexical feature, while failure to repeat exactly can be taken to represent the limits or other representations of the learner's grammatical competence. Consequently, elicited imitation can be used to elicit a potentially very wide range of target structures, both grammatical and nongrammatical.

### 8.2.3.4   Discrete point test

Discrete point tests are constructed on the assumption that language can be divided into components which can be tested successfully. The components are the skills of listening, speaking, reading, writing, and various units of language: phonology, morphology, lexicon, and syntax.

### *Example 8.2*

Researcher: Mackey (1999)

Linguistic structure tested: Question formation

Research questions:

a) Does conversational interaction facilitate second language development?

b) Are the developmental outcomes related to the nature of the conversational interaction and the level of learner involvement?

Methodology:

Participants: thirty-four adult ESL learners (various L1s) (NNS) and six native speakers of English (NS).

Five groups:

a) Interactors (N = 7): NS/NNS pairs participated in a task-based activity in which interaction was allowed.

b) Unready interactors (N = 7): NS/NNS pairs participated in a task-based activity in which interaction was allowed. They differed from the interactor group in that they were less developed than it in terms of English question formation.

c) Observers (N = 7): NNS who only observed an interaction (but did not participate).

d) Scripted (N = 6): NS/NNS pairs participated in the same task, but the input from the NSs was pre-modified.

e) Control (N = 7): No treatment.

Procedure: Seven sessions

a) Pre-test;

b) three treatment sessions—on the three days subsequent to the pre-test;

c) three post-tests—one on the day following the last treatment session, one one week after the first post-test, and one three weeks after the second post-test.

Results:

a) The interactor groups showed greater improvement than the other groups;

b) All groups increased the number of higher-level questions but only the two interactor groups and the script group maintained the increase in all post-tests.

Conclusion: Interaction led to development and more active involvement led to greater development.

### Example 8.3

Researcher: Liu (2018)

Focus: young Chinese EFL learners' anxiety levels and causes for their anxiety in English speaking class.

Research questions:

a) To what degree are the young learners of English anxious when speaking English in class?

b) What causes the students to be anxious when speaking English in class?

c) What are the effects of anxiety on students' English speaking test performance?

d) What are the differences in English speaking anxiety among 7th, 8th and 9th graders?

Methodology:

Participants: A total of 199 (103 male and 96 female) students aged 12 to 16 of this school participated in the research: 74 7th graders, 70 8th graders and 55 9th graders.

Instruments:

a) an adapted 15-item English Speaking Class Anxiety Scale adapted from Horwitz et al.'s (1986) 33-item Foreign Language Classroom Anxiety Scale;

b) semi-structured interview;

c) the final-term English speaking test: 1-minute recitation of a text and a 2-minute teacher-student conversation.

Procedure: A consent was obtained from the teachers, students and their guardians first, then a week prior to the final-term speaking test, the questionnaire and a background information questionnaire were administered to the students in class.

Results:

a) Each sample graders were not anxious when speaking English in class;

b) Students became anxious due to such reasons as peer pressure, fear of making mistakes, fear of losing face, little/no preparation, little practice, task difficulty, and a limited vocabulary;

c) Anxiety seemed to have a negative effect on students' English speaking performance;

d) There were differences in English speaking anxiety levels, as well as in the causes and effects of anxiety among the learners in different grades.

Conclusion: Anxiety is an important factor affecting students' learning of speaking English.

## 8.3 Data analysis

Quantitative data are often analyzed in light of various categorial and probabilistic properties. For example, softwares like SPSS, R, and AMOS are often used to calculate percentages and means to describe patterns and run t-test analyses and ANOVA to explore differences and effects.

Qualitative data are often analyzed according to a certain coding framework (see Table 8.4), or in terms of themes, which can be a word, an idea, a unit, a concept, a sentence or a text (Richards, 2009).

**Table 8.4    A sample error coding & classification scheme** (Liu, 2021)

| Mechanical errors (ME) | |
|---|---|
| ME1 | Misspellings |
| ME2 | Punctuation errors |
| ME3 | Capitalization errors |
| **Syntactical errors (SE)** | |
| SE1 | Errors in part of speech (noun/adj./adv./prep./pron./conj./verb) |
| SE2 | Tense errors |
| SE3 | Errors in agreement |
| SE4 | Verb errors |
| SE5 | Adjective/adverb degree errors |
| SE6 | Articles errors |
| SE7 | Errors in the use of plural or singular forms/uncountable nouns |
| SE8 | Case errors |
| SE9 | Errors in mood /auxiliaries (including modal auxiliaries) |
| **Syntactical errors (SE)** | |
| SE10 | Errors in word order (positive and negative sentence / questions / subordinate clause / adverbs and adjectives) |
| SE11 | Errors in coordinating conjunctions and subordinating conjunctions |
| **Syntactical errors (SE)** | |
| SE12 | Errors of illogical comparison or ill parallelism |
| SE13 | Errors of sentence fragments / run-on sentences / dangling modifiers |
| SE14 | Errors of mixed or confused expressions and sentence structures |
| SE15 | Missing a part of the sentence |
| SE16 | Overuse of a part of the sentence |
| **Lexical errors (LE)** | |
| LE1 | Errors in word formation |
| LE2 | Errors in word choice |
| LE3 | Errors in collocations |
| LE4 | Unclear or incomplete expressions |

# Tasks

## 1. Explain the following terms.

classroom observation    structured interview  story-retelling      discourse completion

oral proficiency interview  stimulated recall      elicited production  discrete point test

## 2. Discuss the following questions.

1) What are the advantages and disadvantages of collecting naturalistic data?

2) What should you pay attention to when doing an interview?

3) What are the advantages and disadvantages of SOPI?

4) What can decision tasks be used for?

5) What are the advantages of survey data?

6) Suppose you want to examine how Chinese students learn past tense in English. What type of data do you need to collect? What methods are you going to use? Why?

## 3. Projects.

1) With reference to Example 8.2, design a similar study.

2) With reference to Example 8.3, design a similar study.

3) Focus on a topic you are interested in, read related literature and select an appropriate method or methods to design the research.

# References

Adams, M. 1978. Methodology for examining second language acquisition. In E. Hatch (Ed.), *Second Language Acquisition: A Book of Readings*. Rowley, MA: Newbury House, 278–296.

Alexander, K. C. & Leung, M. B. B. S. 1999. Evaluation and management of the child with speech delay. *American Family Physician, 59*(11): 3121–3128.

Anandan, K. N. 2014. Teacher talk in the second language classroom. *Language and Language Teaching, 3*(1): 20–24.

Atherton, J. S. 2013. *Language Codes*. Doceo. Retrieved October 3, 2022.

Aubrey, J. S. & Harrison, K. 2004. The gender-role content of children's favorite television programs and its links to their gender-related perceptions. *Media Psychology, 6*(2): 111–146.

Austin, J. L. 1962. *How to Do Things with Words* (2nd ed.). In J. O. Urmson & M. Sbisá (Eds.). Cambridge, MA: Harvard University Press.

Baddeley, A. & Hitch, G. J. 1974. Working memory. In G. Bower (Ed.), *The Psychology of Learning and Motivation: Advances in Research and Theory*. New York: Academic Press, 47–89.

Bailey, K. M. 1983. Competitiveness and anxiety in adult second language learning: Looking at and through the dairy studies. In H. W. Seliger & M. H. Long (Eds.), *Classroom Oriented Research in Second Language Acquisition*. Rowley, MA: Newbury House Publishers, 67–103.

Belmechri, F. & Hummel, K. 1998. Orientations and motivation in the acquisition of English as a second language among high school students in Quebec city. *Language Learning, 48*(2): 219–244.

Benati, A. 2016. Input manipulation, enhancement and processing: Theoretical views and empirical research. *Studies in Second Language Learning and Teaching, 6*(1): 5–88.

Benati, A. & Lee, J. F. 2008. *Grammar Acquisition and Processing Instruction: Secondary and Cumulative Effects*. Clevedon: Multilingual Matters.

Bennett-Kastor, T. 1988. *Analyzing Children's Language: Methods and Theories*. Oxford: Blackwell.

Bernstein, B. 1971. *Class, Codes and Control: Volume 1—Theoretical Studies Towards a Sociology of*

*Language*. London: Psychology Press.

Bialystok, E. & Smith, M. S. 1985. Interlanguage is not a state of mind: An evaluation of the construct for second language acquisition. *Applied Linguistics*, *6*(2): 101–107.

Binet, A. & Simon, T. 1912. *A Method of Measuring the Development of the Intelligence of Young Children*. Chicago: Chicago Medical Book Company.

Bley-Vroman, R. 1989. What is the logical problem of foreign language learning? In S. M. Gass & J. Schachter (Eds.), *Linguistic Perspectives on Second Language Acquisition*. Cambridge: Cambridge University Press, 41–68.

Bloch, B. & Trager, G. L. 1942. *Outline of Linguistic Analysis*. Baltimore: Linguistic Society of America, Waverly Press.

Boudreau, C., MacIntyre, P. & Dewaele, J. M. 2018. Enjoyment and anxiety in second language communication: An idiodynamic approach. *Studies in Second Language Learning and Teaching*, *8*(1): 149–170.

Brown, H. D. 1987. *Principles of Language Learning and Teaching* (2nd ed.). Englewood Ciffs, NJ: Prentice Hall.

Brown, H. D. 1994. *Principles of Language Learning and Teaching*. Englewood Ciffs, NJ: Prentice Hall.

Brown, S. & Attardo, S. 2008. *Understanding Language Structure, Interaction, and Variation* (2nd ed.). Ann Arbor, MI: The University of Michigan Press.

Bruton, A. & Samuda, V. 1980. Learner and teacher roles in the treatment of error in group work. *RELC Journal*, *11*(2): 49–63.

Carroll, J. B. 1981. Twenty-five years of research on foreign language aptitude. In K. Diller (Ed.), *Individual Differences and Universals in Language Learning Aptitude*. Rowley, MA: Newbury House, 83–118.

Carroll, J. & Sapon, S. 2002. Modern language aptitude test. Bethesda, MD: Second Language Testing.

Celce-Murcia, M., Dörnyei, Z. & Thurrell, S. 1997. Direct approaches in L2 instruction: A turning point in communicative language teaching? *TESOL Quarterly*, *31*(1): 141–152.

Chamot, A. U. 1987. The learning strategies of ESL students. In A. Wenden & J. Rubin (Eds.), *Learner Strategies in Language Learning*. Englewood Cliffs, NJ: Prentice Hall, 71–85.

Chandler, D. 2004. *Semiotics: The Basics*. London: Routledge.

Chang, C. B. & Mishler, A. 2012. Evidence for language transfer leading to a perceptual advantage for non-native listeners. *The Journal of the Acoustical Society of America*, *132*(4): 2700–2710.

Chastain, K. 1975. Affective and ability factors in second language learning. *Language Learning*, *25*(1): 153–161.

Chaudron, C. 2003. Data collection in SLA research. In C. Doughty & M. H. Long (Eds.), *The Handbook of Second Language Acquisition*. Oxford: Blackwell, 762–828.

Cherry, K. Alfred Binet and the history of IQ testing. *Verywell Mind*. Retrieved April 13, 2022, from verywellmind website.

Chomsky, N. 1972. *Language and Mind*. New York: Harcourt Brace Jovanovich.

Chomsky, N. 1975. *Reflections on Language*. New York: Pantheon.

Chomsky, N. 1981. *Lectures on Government and Binding*. Berlin: De Gruyter.

Chomsky, N. 1986. *Knowledge of Language: Its Nature, Origin and Use*. New York: Praeger.

Chouinard, M. M. & Clark, E. V. 2003. Adult reformulation of child errors as negative evidence. *Journal of Child Language, 30*: 637–669.

Clahsen, H. & Muysken, P. 1989. The UG paradox in L2 acquisition. *Second Language Research, 5*(1): 1–29.

Clark, U. 2013. *Language and Identity in Englishes*. London: Routledge.

Clément, R., Dörnyei, Z. & Noels, K. A. 1994. Motivation, self-confidence, and group cohesion in the foreign language. *Language Learning, 44*(3): 417–448.

Coplan, J. 1985. Evaluation of the child with delayed speech or language. *Pediatric Annals, 14*: 203–208.

Cronbach, L. & Snow, R. 1977. *Aptitudes and Instructional Methods: A Handbook for Research on Interactions*. New York: Irvington Publishers.

Crystal, D. 1992. *An Encyclopedic Dictionary of Language and Languages*. Oxford: Blackwell.

De Saussure, F. 1983. *Course in General Linguistics* (R. Harris, Trans.). London: Duckworth (Original work published in 1916).

Deci, E. & Ryan, R. M. 1985. *Intrinsic Motivation and Self-determination in Human Behavior*. New York: Plenum Press.

DeKeyser, R. M. 1997. Beyond explicit rule learning: Automatizing second language morphosyntax. *Studies in Second Language Acquisition, 19*(2): 195–221.

Dewaele, J. M. & MacIntyre, P. D. 2014. The two faces of Janus? Anxiety and enjoyment in the foreign language classroom. *Studies in Second Language Learning and Teaching 4*(2): 237–274.

Dewar, G. Baby talk 101: How infant-directed speech helps babies learn language. *Parenting Science*. Retrieved October, 2013, from ParentingScience website.

Dewar, K. M. & Xu, F. 2010. Induction, overhypothesis, and the origin of abstract knowledge: Evidence from 9-month-old infants. *Psychological Science, 21*(12): 1871–1877.

Dirven, R. & Verspoor, M. 2004. *Cognitive Exploration of Language and Linguistics*. Amsterdam: John Benjamins.

Dong, L., Liu, M. & Yang, F. 2022. The relationship between foreign language classroom anxiety, enjoyment, and expectancy-value motivation. and their predictive effects on Chinese high school students' self-rated foreign language proficiency. *Frontiers in Psychology*, 13:860603.

Donnelly, C. E. 1994. *Linguistics for Writers*. Albany: State University of New York Press.

Dorval, B. (Ed.) 1990. *Conversational Organization and Its Development: Advances in Discourse Processes Volume XXXVIII*. Norwood: Ablex.

Doughty, C. & Williams, J. (Eds.). 1998. *Focus on Form in Classroom Second Language Acquisition*. Cambridge: Cambridge University Press.

Dörnyei, Z. 1990. Conceptualizing motivation in foreign language learning. *Language Learning, 40*(1): 45–78.

Dörnyei, Z. 2005. *The Psychology of the Language Learner: Individual Differences in Second Language Acquisition*. Mahwah: Lawrence Erlbaum Associates.

Dörnyei, Z. 2009. The L2 motivational self system. In Z. Dörnyei & E. Ushioda (Eds.), *Motivation, Language Identity and the L2 Self*. Bristol: Multilingual Matters, 9–42.

Dulay, H. C. & Burt, M. K. 1974. Natural sequences in child second language acquisition. *Language Learning, 24*(1): 37–53.

Eckman, F. R. 1977. Markedness and the contrastive analysis hypothesis. *Language Learning, 27*(2): 315–330.

Ellis, N. C. & Wulff, S. 2015. Second language acquisition. In E. Dabrowska & D. Divjak (Eds.), *Handbook of Cognitive Linguistics*. Berlin: De Gruyter, 409–716.

Ellis, R. 1985. *Understanding Second Language Acquisition*. Oxford: Oxford University Press.

Ellis, R. 1991. The Interaction Hypothesis: A critical evaluation. ERIC Document Reproduction Service No. ED338037.

Ellis, R. 1994. *The Study of Second Language Acquisition*. Oxford: Oxford University Press.

Ellis, R. 2003. *Task-Based Language Learning and Teaching*. Oxford: Oxford University Press.

Ellis, R. 2016. Focus on form: A critical review. *Language Teaching Research, 20*(3): 405–428.

Ewald, J. D. 2007. Foreign language learning anxiety in upper-level classes: Involving students as researchers. *Foreign Language Annals, 40*(1): 122–142.

Fairclough, N. 1995. *Critical Discourse Analysis*. London: Longman.

Farahani, A. A. K., Mehrdad, A. G. & Ahghar, M. R. 2014. Access to universal grammar in adult second language acquisition. *Procedia-Social and Behavioral Sciences, 136*: 298–301.

Fathman, A. 1975. The relationship between age and second language productive ability. *Language Learning, 25*(2): 245–253.

Ferguson, C. A. 1975. Toward a characterization of English foreigner talk. *Anthropological Linguistics, 17*: 1–14.

Fernández, C. 2011. Approaches to grammar instruction in teaching materials: A study in current L2 beginning-level Spanish textbooks. *Hispania, 94*(1): 155–170.

Field, J. 2007. *Psycholinguistics: The Key Concepts*. London: Routledge.

Foster, P. 1999. Task-based learning and pedagogy. *ELT Journal, 53*: 69–70.

Fuchs, A. 2002. *The Critical Period Hypothesis Supported by Genie's Case*. Munich: GRIN Verlag.

Gaies, S. 1979. Linguistic input in first and second language learning. In F. R. Eckman & A. J. Hastings (Eds.), *Studies in First and Second Language Acquisition*. Rowley, MA: Newbury House, 185–193.

Gao, Y., Zhao, Y., Cheng, Y. & Zhou, Y. 2004. Motivation types of Chinese university students. *Asian Journal of English Language Teaching, 14*: 45–64.

Gardner, H. 1983. *Frames of Mind: The Theory of Multiple Intelligences*. New York: Basic Books.

Gardner, H. 1987. The theory of multiple intelligences. *Annals of Dyslexia, 37*: 19–35.

Gardner, R. C. 1985. *Social Psychology and Second Language Learning: The Role of Attitudes and Motivation*. London: Edward Arnold.

Gardner, R. C. & Lambert, W. E. 1972. *Attitudes and Motivation in Second Language Learning*. Rowley, MA: Newbury House.

Gardner, R. C. & MacIntyre, P. D. 1993. A student's contributions to second language learning, Part II: Affective variables. *Language Teaching, 26*: 1–11.

Gardner, R. C., Lalonde, R. N. & Moorcroft, R. 1985. The role of attitudes and motivation in second language learning: Correlational and experimental considerations. *Language Learning, 35*(2): 207–227.

Gass, S. 1997. *Input, Interaction, and the Second Language Learner*. Mahwah, NJ: Lawrence Erlbaum.

Gass, S. M. 2003. Input and interaction. In C. J. Doughty & M. H. Long (Eds.), *The Handbook of Second Language Acquisition*. Malden, MA: Blackwell, 224–255.

Ghonchepour, M. & Moghaddam, M. P. 2018. The role of intelligence in learning English as a foreign language. *Research in English Language Pedagogy, 6*(1): 25–38.

Gleitman, L. R. & Newport, E. L. 1995. The invention of language by children: Environmental and biological influences on the acquisition of language. In L. R. Gleitman & M. Liberman (Eds.), *An Invitation to Cognitive Science* Vol. 1 (2nd ed.). Cambridge, MA: MIT Press, 1–24.

Green, J. M. & Oxford, R. 1995. A closer look at learning strategies, L2 proficiency, and gender. *TESOL Quarterly, 29*(2): 261–297.

Gregersen, T. S. & Horwitz, E. K. 2002. Language learning and perfectionism: Anxious and nonanxious language learners' reactions to their own oral performance. *Modern Language Journal, 86*(4): 562–570.

Grice, P. 1975. Logic and conversation. In P. Cole & J. Morgan (Eds.), *Syntax and Semantics 3: Speech Acts*. New York: Academic Press, 41–58.

Gürsoy, E. & Akin, F. 2013. Is younger really better? Anxiety about learning a foreign language in Turkish children. *Social Behavior and Personality: An International Journal, 41*(5): 827–841.

Habók, A. & Magyar, A. 2018. The effect of language learning strategies on proficiency, attitudes and school achievement. *Frontiers in Psychology, 8*: 2358.

Hafiz, F. M. & Tudor, I. 1989. Extensive reading and the development of language skills. *ELT Journal, 43*(1): 4–13.

Hakuta, K. 1976. A case study of a Japanese child learning English as a second language. *Language Learning, 26*(2): 321–351.

Halliday, M. A. K. 1964. Comparison and translation. In M. A. K. Halliday, M. McIntosh & P. Strevens (Eds.), *The Linguistic Sciences and Language Teaching*. London: Longman, 111–134.

Han, Z. 2005. Input Enhancement: Untangling the Tangles. Keynote presentation. *27th Winter Applied Linguistics Conference*, New York, United States.

Harley, T. A. 2001. *The Psychology of Language: From Data to Theory* (2nd ed.). Hove: Psychology Press.

Hernández, T. A. 2010. The relationship among motivation, interaction, and the development of second language oral proficiency in a study-abroad context. *The Modern Language Journal, 94*(4): 600–617.

Horwitz, E. K., Horwitz, M. B. & Cope, J. 1986. Foreign language classroom anxiety. *The Modern Language Journal, 70*(2): 125–132.

Hosseini, B. S. & Pourmandnia, D. 2013. Language learners' attitudes and beliefs: Brief review of the related literature and frameworks. *International Journal on New Trends in Education and Their Applications, 4*(4): 63–74.

Humphreys, G. & Spratt, M. 2008. Many languages, many motivations: A study of Hong Kong students' motivation to learn different target languages. *System, 36*(2): 313–335.

Humphries, T., Kushalnagar, P., Mathur, G., Napoli, D. J., Padden, C., Rathmann, C. & Smith, S. R. 2012. Language acquisition for deaf children: Reducing the harms of zero tolerance to the use of alternative approaches. *Harm Reduction Journal, 9*: 16.

Hunt, K. W. 1970. Syntactic maturity in school-children and adults. *Monographs of the Society for Research in Child Development, 35*(1): iii–iv, 1–67.

Irvine, M. 2014. Introduction to linguistics and symbolic systems: Key concepts. Georgetown University. Retrieved August 25, 2021 from google website.

Jarvis, S. & Pavlenko, A. 2008. *Crosslinguistic influence in language and cognition*. New York: Routledge.

Joos, M. 1961. *The Five Clocks: A Linguistic Excursion into the Five Styles of English Usage.* New York: Harcourt, Brace & World.

Kaushanskaya, M. & Marian, V. 2009. The bilingual advantage in novel word learning. *Psychonomic Bulletin & Review, 16*(4): 705–710.

Kim, Y. 2012. Task complexity, learning opportunities and Korean EFL learner's question development. *Studies in Second Language Acquisition, 34*(4): 627–658.

Kleinmann, H. H. 1977. Avoidance behavior in adult second language acquisition. *Language Learning, 27*(1): 93–107.

Krashen, S. 1981. *Second Language Acquisition and Second Language Learning.* Oxford: Pergamon Press.

Krashen, S. 1982. *Principles and Practice in Second Language Acquisition.* Oxford: Pergamon Press.

Krashen, S. 1985. *The Input Hypothesis: Issues and Implications.* London: Longman.

Krashen, S. 1989. We acquire vocabulary and spelling by reading: Additional evidence for the input hypothesis. *The Modern Language Journal, 73*(4): 440–464.

Krashen, S. 1998. Comprehensible output? *System, 26*(2): 175–182.

Krashen, S. 2011. The compelling (not just interesting) input hypothesis. *The English Connection, 15*(3): 1.

Krashen, S. & Terrell, T. D. 1983. *The Natural Approach: Language Acquisition in the Classroom.* Hayward, CA: The Alemany Press.

Kumaravadivelu, B. 2006. *Understanding Language Teaching: From Method to Postmethod.* New York: Routledge.

Labov, W. 1966. *The Social Stratification of English in New York City.* Washington: Center for Applied Linguistics.

Labov, W. 1969. The logic of nonstandard English. *Georgetown Monographs on Language and Linguistics, 22*: 1–31.

Lado, R. 1957. *Linguistics across Cultures: Applied Linguistics for Language Teachers.* Ann Arbor, MI: University of Michigan Press.

Lakoff, R. 1975. *Language and Woman's Place: Text and Commentaries*. New York: Oxford University Press.

Lee, I. 2017. *Classroom Writing Assessment and Feedback in L2 School Contexts*. Singapore: Springer.

Lee, J. F. & Benati, A. 2007. *Second Language Processing: An Analysis of Theory, Problems and Solutions*. London: Continuum.

Leow, R. P. 1997. Attention, awareness, and foreign language behavior. *Language Learning, 47*(3): 467–505.

Leow, R. P. 2000. A study of the role of awareness in foreign language behavior: Aware versus unaware learners. *Studies in Second Language Acquisition, 22*(4): 557–584.

Leow, R. P. 2001. Do learners notice enhanced forms while interacting with the L2? An online and offline study of the role of written input enhancement in L2 reading. *Hispania, 84*(3): 496–509.

Leung, A. K., Robson, W. L., Fagan, J., Chopra, S. & Lim, S. H. 1995. Mental retardation. *Journal of the Royal Society of Health, 115*(1): 31–39.

Li, C. & Wei, L. 2023. Anxiety, enjoyment, and boredom in language learning amongst junior secondary students in rural China: How do they contribute to L2 achievement?. *Studies in Second Language Acquisition, 45*: 93–108.

Li, S. 2015. The associations between language aptitude and second language grammar acquisition: A meta-analytic review of five decades of research. *Applied Linguistics, 36*(3): 385–408.

Lightbown, P. M. 1998. The importance of timing in focus on form. In C. Doughty & J. Williams (Eds.), *Focus on Form in Classroom Second Language Acquisition*. Cambridge: Cambridge University Press, 177–196.

Lightbown, P. M. & Spada, N. M. 2006. Explaining second language learning. *How Languages Are Learned* (3rd ed.). Oxford: Oxford University Press, 29–50.

Littlejohn, S. 2002. *Theories of Human Communication* (7th ed.). Belmont, CA: Wadsworth.

Liu, M. 2007. Chinese students' motivation to learn English at the tertiary level. *Asian EFL Journal, 9*(1): 126–146.

Liu, M. 2009. *Reticence and Anxiety in Oral English Lessons*. Bern: Peter Lang AG.

Liu, M. 2016. Interrelations between foreign language listening anxiety and strategy use and their predicting effects on test performance of high- and low-proficient Chinese university EFL learners. *The Asia-Pacific Education Researcher, 25*(4): 647–655.

Liu, M. 2017. Motivation, motivation intensity, use of Chinese and self-rated proficiency in Chinese. *College Student Journal, 51*(1): 63–76.

Liu, M. 2018. Understanding Chinese middle school students' anxiety in English speaking class. *The Journal of Asia TEFL, 15*(3): 721–734.

Liu, M. 2021. Focus and effects of peer and machine feedback on Chinese university EFL learners' revisions of English argumentative essays. *Theory and Practice of Second Language Acquisition*, *7*(1): 75–98.

Liu, M. & Jackson, J. 2008. An exploration of Chinese EFL learners' unwillingness to communicate and foreign language anxiety. *The Modern Language Journal, 92*(1): 71–86.

Liu, M. & Xiangming, L. 2019. Changes in and effects of anxiety on English test performance in Chinese postgraduate EFL classrooms. *Education Research International*, 1: 1-11.

Liu, M. & Yuan, R. 2021. Changes in and effects of foreign language classroom anxiety and listening anxiety on Chinese undergraduate students' English proficiency in the COVID-19 context. *Frontiers in Psychology, 12*: 670824.

Liu, M. 2024. Chinese university students' L2 motivational self: A mixed-method study. *Journal of Asia TEFL*, 21(3): 721–729.

Liu, M., Wu, X. & Yang. F. 2024. Emotions in English language classrooms among Chinese top university students. *Scientific Reports*, 14:20081, 2045–2322.

Loewen, S. 2018. Focus on form versus focus on forms. *The TESOL Encyclopedia of English Language Teaching,* 1–6.

Long, M. H. 1988. Instructed interlanguage development. In L. Beebe (Ed.), *Issues in Second Language Acquisition: Multiple Perspectives*. Rowley, MA: Newbury, 115–141.

Long, M. H. 1991. Focus on form: A design feature in language teaching methodology. In K. de Bot, R. Ginsberg & C. Kramsch (Eds.), *Foreign Language Research in Cross-cultural Perspective*. Amsterdam: John Benjamins, 39–52.

Long, M. H. 1996. The role of the linguistic environment in second language acquisition. In W. Ritchie & T. Bhatia (Eds.), *Handbook of Second Language Acquisition*. San Diego: Academic Press, 413–468.

Long, M. H. 2017. Instructed second language acquisition (ISLA): Geopolitics, methodological issues, and some major research questions. *Instructed Second Language Acquisition, 1*(1): 7–44.

Lowth, R. 1762. *A Short Introduction to English Grammar: With Critical Notes*. London: A. Millar and R . & J. Dodsley.

Lust, B. 2006. *Child Language: Acquisition and Growth*. Cambridge: Cambridge University Press.

Lyons, J. 1981. *Language and Linguistics*. Cambridge: Cambridge University Press.

MacIntyre, P. D. & Gardner, R. C. 1994. The subtle effects of language anxiety on cognitive processing in the second language. *Language Learning, 44*: 283–305.

Mackey, A. 1999. Input, interaction, and second language development: An empirical study of question formation in ESL. *Studies in Second Language Acquisition, 21*(4): 557–587.

Mackey, A. & Philp, J. 1998. Conversational interaction and second language development: Recasts, responses, and red herrings? *Modern Language Journal, 82*(3): 338–356.

Mackey, A., Gass, S. & McDonough, K. 2000. How do learners perceive interactional feedback? *Studies in Second Language Acquisition, 22*(4): 471–497.

MacShane, F. (Ed.). 1981. *Selected Letters of Raymond Chandler.* London: Jonathan Cape.

Malallaha, S. 2000. English in an Arabic environment: Current attitudes to English among Kuwait University students. *International Journal of Bilingual Education and Bilingualism, 3*(1): 19–43.

McDavid, R. I. 1948. Postvocalic /-r/ in South Carolina: A social analysis. *American Speech, 23*: 194–203.

McDonough, K. 2005. Identifying the impact of negative feedback and learners' responses on ESL question development. *Studies in Second Language Acquisition, 27*(1): 79–103.

McLeod, P. J. 1993. What studies of communication with infants ask us about psychology: Baby-talk and other speech registers. *Canadian Psychology/Psychologie Canadienne, 34*(3): 282–292.

McLeod, S. 2020. Behaviourist approach. Retrieved 13 August, 2021, from Simply Psychology website.

Miyake, A. & Friedman, N. P. 1998. Individual differences in second language proficiency: Working memory as "language aptitude". In A. F. Healy & L. E. Bourne (Eds.), *Foreign Language Learning: Psycholinguistic Studies on Training and Retention.* Mahwah, NJ: Lawrence Erlbaum, 339–364.

Miyake, A. & Shah, P. (Eds.). 1999. *Models of Working Memory: Mechanisms of Active Maintenance and Executive Control.* Cambridge: Cambridge University Press.

Monaghan, P., Shillcock, R. C., Christiansen, M. H. & Kirby, S. 2014. How arbitrary is language? *Philosophical Transactions of the Royal Society B, 369*(1651): 20130299.

Montrul, S. 2009. Reexaming the fundamental difference hypothesis: What can early bilinguals tell us? *Studies in Second Language Acquisition, 31*(2): 225–257.

Mulac, A., Bradac, J. J. & Karol, M. S. 1985. Male/female language differences and attributional consequences in children's television. *Human Communication Research, 11*(4): 481–506.

Mulder, J. & Hervey, S. 1975. Language as a system of systems. *La Linguistique, 11*(2): 3–22.

Ng, S. & Deng, F. 2017. Language and power. *Oxford Research Encyclopedia of Communication.* Retrieved from Oxford University Press website.

Nitschke, S., Kidd, E. & Serratrice, L. 2010. First language transfer and long-term structural priming in comprehension. *Language and Cognitive Processes, 25*(1): 94–114.

Nordquist, R. 2020. Defining synchronic linguistics. Retrieved August 17, 2021, from ThoughtCo website.

Norris, J. M. & Ortega, L. 2000. Effectiveness of L2 instruction: A research synthesis and quantitative meta-analysis. *Language Learning, 50*(3): 417–528.

Norris, J. & Ortega, L. 2003. Defining and measuring SLA. In C. Doughty & M. H. Long (Eds.), *The Handbook of Second Language Acquisition*. Malden, MA: Blackwell, 717–761.

O'Grady, W., Archibald, J. & Katamba, F. (Eds.). 2011. *Contemporary Linguistics: An Introduction* (2nd ed.). Boston: Pearson.

Ollerhead, S. & Oostuizen, J. 2005. Meaning-focused versus form-focused L2 instruction: Implications for writing educational materials for South African learners of English. *Stellenbosch Papers in Linguistics, 36*: 59–84.

O'Malley, J. M., Chamot, A. U., Stewner-Manzanares, Kupper, L. & Russo, R. P. 1985. Learning strategies used by beginning and intermediate ESL students. *Language Learning, 35*(1): 21–46.

Ottenheimer, H. J. 2009. *The Anthropology of Language: An Introduction to Linguistic Anthropology* (2nd ed.). Belmont, CA: Wadsworth Cengage Learning.

Oxford, R. L. 1990. *Language Learning Strategies*. Boston: Heinle & Heinle Publishers.

Petrey, S. 1990. *Speech Acts and Literary Theory*. London: Routledge.

Phan, T. M. U., Ly, T. T., Nguyen, T. T. H. & Nguyen, N. M. L. 2020. The relationship between learning strategy use in English and motivation of students at a college in Can Tho city, Vietnam. *European Journal of English Language Teaching*, 6(1): 130–200.

Pienemann, M. 1987. Determining the influence of instruction on L2 speech processing. *Australian Review of Applied Linguistics, 10*(2): 83–113.

Pienemann, M. 1989. Is language teachable? Psycholinguistic experiments and hypotheses. *Applied Linguistics, 10*(1): 52–79.

Pinker, S. 2007. *The Language Instinct: How the Mind Creates Language*. New York: Harper Perennial Modern Classics.

Porter, L. W. & Duncan, C. P. 1953. Negative transfer in verbal learning. *Journal of Experimental Psychology, 46*(1): 61–64.

Ramat, G. A., Mauri, C. & Molinelli, P. (Eds.). 2013. *Synchrony and Diachrony: A Dynamic Interface*. Amsterdam: John Benjamins, 17–18.

Reid, T. B. 1956. Linguistics, structuralism, philology. *Archivum Linguisticum, 8*(1): 28–37.

Richards, L. 2009. *Handling Qualitative Data: A Practical Guide*. Los Angeles: Sage.

Roberson, D., Davies, I. & Davidoff, J. 2000. Colour categories are not universal: Replications and new evidence from a Stone-Age culture. *Journal of Experimental Psychology: General, 129*(3): 369–398.

Rubin, J. 1987. Learner strategies: Theoretical assumptions, research, history, and typology. In A. Wenden & J. Rubin (Eds.), *Learner Strategies in Language Learning*. Englewood Cliffs, NJ: Prentice Hall, 15–30.

Ruhl, C. 2020. Intelligence: Definition, theories and testing. *Cognitive Psychology*. Retrieved August 3, 2021, from simplypsychology website.

Sacks, H. 1995. *Lectures on Conversation*. Oxford: Blackwell.

Sacks, H., Schegloff, E. A. & Jefferson, G. 1974. A simplest systematics for the organization of turn-taking for conversation. *Language, 50*(4): 696–735.

Salehi, M. & Sadighi, F. 2012. The relationship between intelligence and foreign language learning, and the role of practice. *Journal of Language, Culture, and Translation (LCT), 1*(1): 33–48.

Sapir, E. 1921. *Language*. New York: Harcourt Brace.

Saxton, M., Backley, P. & Gallaway, C. 2005. Negative input for grammatical errors: Effects after a lag of 12 weeks. *Journal of Child Language, 32*(3): 643–672.

Schachter, J. 1988. Second language acquisition and its relationship to Universal Grammar. *Applied Linguistics, 9*(3): 219–235.

Schachter, J. 1989. Testing a proposed universal. In S. Gass & J. Schachter (Eds.), *Linguistic Perspectives on Second Language Acquisition*. Cambridge: Cambridge University Press, 73–88.

Schegloff, E. 1992. Introduction. In H. Sacks (Ed.), *Lectures on Conversation* (Vol. 1). Oxford: Blackwell, ix–lxii.

Schegloff, E. A., Jefferson, G. & Sacks, H. 1977. The preference for self-correction in the organisation of repair in conversation. *Language, 53*(2): 361–382.

Schmidt, R. W. 1990. The role of consciousness in second language learning. *Applied Linguistics, 11*(2): 129–158.

Schmidt, R. W. 1994. Deconstructing consciousness in search of useful definitions for applied linguistics. *AILA Review, 11*: 11–26.

Schmidt, R. W. 2001. Attention. In P. Robinson (Ed.), *Cognition and Second Language Instruction*. Cambridge: Cambridge University Press, 3–32.

Schmidt, R. W. 2012. Attention, awareness, and individual differences in language learning. In W. Chan, K. Chin, S. Bhatt & I. Walker (Eds.), *Perspectives on Individual Characteristics and Foreign Language Education: Studies in Second and Foreign Language Education*. Berlin: De Gruyter, 27–50.

Schmidt, R. W. & Frota, S. N. 1986. Developing basic conversational ability in a second language: A case study of an adult learner of Portuguese. In R. R. Day (Ed.), *Talking to Learn: Conversation in Second Language Acquisition*. Rowley, MA: Newbury, 237–326.

Schumann, J. H. 1978. *The Pidginization Process: A Model for Second Language Acquisition*. Rowley, MA: Newbury.

Schwartz, B. 1997. On the basis of the Basic Variety. *Second Language Research, 13*: 386–402.

Schwartz, E. R. 1990. Speech and language disorders. In M. W. Schwartz (Ed.), *Pediatric Primary Care: A Problem Oriented Approach*. St. Louis: Mosby, 696–700.

Selikowitz, M. 1998. *Dyslexia and Other Learning Difficulties: The Facts* (2nd ed). Oxford: Oxford University Press.

Selinker, L. 1972. Interlanguage. *International Review of Applied Linguistics in Language Teaching, 10*: 209–231.

Service, E. & Kohonen, V. 1995. Is the relation between phonological memory and foreign language learning accounted for by vocabulary acquisition? *Applied Psycholinguistics, 16*(2): 155–172.

Sharwood Smith, M. 1993. Input enhancement in instructed SLA studies: Theoretical bases. *Studies in Second Language Acquisition, 15*(2): 165–179.

Shatz, I. 2016. Native language influence during second language acquisition: A large-scale learner corpus analysis. In M. Hirakawa, J. Matthews, K. Otaki, N. Snape & M. Umeda (Eds.), *Proceedings of the Pacific Second Language Research Forum (PacSLRF 2016)*. Japan Second Language Association, 175–180.

Shintani, N. 2013. The effect of focus on form and focus on forms instruction on the acquisition of productive knowledge of L2 vocabulary by young beginning-level learners. *TESOL Quarterly, 47*(1): 36–62.

Shirvan, M. E. & Taherian, T. 2021. Longitudinal examination of university students' foreign language enjoyment and foreign language classroom anxiety in the course of general English: Latent growth curve modeling. *International Journal of Bilingual Education and Bilingualism, 24*(1): 31–49.

Shojaei, E., Jafari, Z. & Gholami, M. 2016. Effect of early intervention on language development in hearing-impaired children. *Iranian Journal of Otorhinolaryngology, 28*(1): 13–21.

Shore, R. 1997. *Rethinking the Brain: New Insights into Early Development*. New York: Families and Work Institute.

Sidnell, J. 2016. Conversation analysis. *Oxford Research Encyclopedias*: *Linguistics*. Retrieved from Oxford University Press website.

Skehan, P. 1989. *Individual Differences in Second Language Learning*. London: Edward Arnold.

Skinner, B. F. 1966. What is the experimental analysis of behavior? *Journal of the Experimental Analysis of Behavior, 9*(3): 213–218.

Song, H. S. & Schwartz, B. D. 2009. Testing the fundamental difference hypothesis: L2 adult, L2 child, and L1 child comparisons in the acquisition of Korean "w"-constructions with negative polarity items. *Studies in Second Language Acquisition, 31*(2): 323–361.

Sonja, E. 2010. *Talking to children: The role of child-directed speech in language development* [Paper presentation]. The Language Learning Cafe, Colchester, UK.

Spada, N. & Lightbown, P. 1999. Instruction, first language influence and developmental readiness in second language acquisition. *The Modern Language Journal, 83*(1): 1–22.

Spearman, C. 1904. "General intelligence" objectively determined and measured. *American Journal of Psychology, 15*(2): 201–292.

Spielberger, C. D. 1983. *Manual for the State-trait Anxiety Inventory*. Palo Alto, CA: Consulting Psychologists Press.

Spolsky, B. 2000. Anniversary article language motivation revisited. *Applied Linguistics, 21*(2): 157–169.

Sternberg, R. J. 1985. *Beyond IQ: A Triarchic Theory of Human Intelligence*. Cambridge: Cambridge University Press..

Sternberg, R. J. 1997. The concept of intelligence and its role in lifelong learning and success. *American Psychologist, 52*(10): 1030–1037.

Sternberg, R. J. 2003. Contemporary theories of intelligence. In W. M. Reynolds & G. E. Miller (Eds.), *Handbook of Psychology: Educational Psychology* (Vol. 7). Hoboken, NJ: John Wiley & Sons Inc, 23–45.

Strong, M. 1984. Integrative motivation: Cause or result of successful second language acquisition. *Language Learning, 34*(3): 1–14.

Swain, M. 1985. Communicative competence: Some roles of comprehensible input and comprehensible output in its development. In S. Gass & C. Madden (Eds.), *Input in Second Language Acquisition*. Rowley, MA: Newbury House, 235–253.

Swain, M. & Lapkin, S. 1995. Problems in output and the cognitive processes they generate: A step towards second language learning. *Applied Linguistics, 16*(3): 371–391.

Thiessen, E. D., Hill, E. A. & Saffran, J. R. 2005. Infant-directed speech facilitates word segmentation. *Infancy, 7*(1): 53–71.

Thomson, G. 1947. Charles Spearman, 1863–1945. *The Royal Society, 5*(15): 373–385.

Thurstone, L. L. 1938. *Primary Mental Abilities*. Chicago: University of Chicago Press.

Todd, A. D. 1993. A diagnosis of doctor-patient discourse in the prescription of contraception. In S. Fisher & A. A. Todd (Eds.), *The Social Organization of Doctor-Patient Communication*. Norwood, NJ: Ablex, 183–212.

Tomasello, M. & Kruger, A. C. 1992. Joint attention in action: Acquiring verbs in ostensive and nonostensive contexts. *Journal of Child Language, 19*(2): 311–333.

Trudell, B. 2005. Language choice, education and community identity. *International Journal of Educational Development, 25*(3): 237–251.

Trudgill, P. 1992. *Introducing Language and Society.* London: Penguin.

Truscott, J. 1998. Noticing in second language acquisition: A critical review. *Second Language Research, 14*(2): 103–135.

Truscott, J. 2004. The effectiveness of grammar instruction: Analysis of a meta-analysis. *English Teaching and Learning, 28*(3): 17–29.

Ur, P. 1996. *A Course in Language Teaching: Practice and Theory.* Cambridge: Cambridge University Press.

VanPatten, B. 1993. Grammar teaching for the acquisition-rich classroom. *Foreign Language Annals, 26*: 433–450.

VanPatten, B. 1995. Cognitive aspects of input processing in second language acquisition. In P. Heshemipour, R. Maldonado & M. van Naerssen (Eds.), *Studies in Language Learning and Spanish Linguistics.* New York: McGraw-Hill, 170–183.

VanPatten, B. 1996. *Input Processing and Grammar Instruction: Theory and Research.* Norwood, NJ: Ablex.

VanPatten, B. 2000. Processing instruction as form-meaning connections: Issues in theory and research. In J. Lee & A. Valdman (Eds.), *Form and Meaning: Multiple Perspectives.* Boston: Heinle & Heinle Publishers, 43–68.

VanPatten, B. 2004. Input processing in SLA. In B. VanPatten (Ed.), *Processing Instruction: Theory, Research, and Commentary.* Mahwah, NJ: Lawrence Erlbaum, 5–31.

VanPatten, B. 2007. Input processing in adult second language acquisition. In B. VanPatten & J. Williams (Eds.), *Theories in Second Language Acquisition.* Mahwah, NJ: Lawrence Erlbaum, 115–135.

VanPatten, B. 2008. Processing matters in input enhancement. In T. Piske & M. Young-Scholten (Eds.), *Input Matters in SLA.* Bristol: Multilingual Matters, 47–61.

VanPatten, B. 2010. *Key Terms in Second Language Acquisition.* London: Continuum.

VanPatten, B. & Cadierno, T. 1993. Explicit instruction and input processing. *Studies in Second Language Acquisition, 15*(2): 225–243.

Varonis, E. M. & Gass, S. 1985. Non-native/non-native conversations: A model for negotiation of meaning. *Applied Linguistics, 6*(1): 71–90.

Vygotsky, L. S. 1978. *Mind in Society: The Development of Higher Psychological Processes.* Cambridge: Harvard University Press.

Wardhaugh, R. 1977. *Introduction to Linguistics* (2nd ed.). New York: McGraw-Hill.

Wardhaugh, R. 2006. *An Introduction to Sociolinguistics*. Malden, MA: Blackwell.

Watson, J. B. 1913. Psychology as the behaviorist views it. *Psychological Review, 20*(2): 158–177.

Weatherall, A. 2002. *Gender, Language and Discourse*. London: Routledge.

Weinstein, C. E. & Mayer, R. E. 1986. The teaching of learning strategies. In M. C. Wittrock (Ed.), *Handbook of Research on Teaching*. New York: Macmillan, 315–327.

Wenden, A. L. 1985. Learner strategies. *TESOL Newsletter, 19*(5): 1–7.

White, L. 2003. *Second Language Acquisition and Universal Grammar*. Cambridge: Cambridge University Press.

Whorf, B. L. 1956. *Language, Thought and Reality: Selected Writings*. J. B. Carroll (Ed.). London: Chapman & Hall.

Williams, J. 1999. Learner-generated attention to form. *Language Learning, 49*(4): 583–625.

Williams, J. & Evans, J. 1998. What kind of focus and on which form? In C. Doughty & J. Williams (Eds.), *Focus on Form in Classroom Second Language Acquisition*. Cambridge: Cambridge University Press, 139–155.

Williams, J. N. 2004. Implicit learning of form-meaning connections. In B. VanPatten, J. Williams, S. Rott & M. Overstreet (Eds.), *Form-meaning Connections in Second Language Acquisition*. Mahwah, NJ: Lawrence Erlbaum, 203–218.

Wong, W. 2004. The nature of processing instruction. In B. VanPatten (Ed.), *Processing Instruction: Theory, Research, and Commentary*. Mahwah, NJ: Lawrence Erlbaum, 33–65.

Wong, W. 2005. *Input Enhancement: From Theory and Research to the Classroom*. New York: McGraw-Hill.

Wong, W. & VanPatten, B. 2003. The evidence is IN: Drills are out. *Foreign Language Annals, 36*(3): 403–423.

Xiangming, L., Liu, M. & Zhang, C. 2020. Technological impact on language anxiety dynamic. *Computers & Education, 150*: 103839.

Zimmerman, D. H. & West, C. 1975. Sex roles, interruptions and silences in conversation. In B. Thorne & C. West (Eds.), *Language and Sex: Difference and Dominance*. Rowley, MA: Newbury House, 105–129.

党的二十大报告学习辅导百问 . 2022. 北京 : 党建读物出版社 / 学习出版社 .